Good E

You may know of An...
Pretending series of boo...

Anne was a medical doctor and missionary ... for sixteen years, but, during the time she was writing this book, she was in training as a psychotherapist and now works full time as a counsellor. She was one of the first women to be ordained as a priest in the Church of England and serves in her local church as an honorary curate.

When not working, she now has a cast iron excuse for playing like a two-year-old whenever one of her five grandchildren comes to visit.

GOOD ENOUGH
FOR GOD

Anne J. Townsend

TRIANGLE

First published in Great Britain in 1996
Triangle
SPCK
Holy Trinity Church
Marylebone Road
London NW1 4DU

ACKNOWLEDGEMENTS
Bible quotations are from the Revised Standard Version of the Bible
© 1971 and 1952.

We would like to take this opportunity to thank those individuals and
organizations who have given us permission to use and adapt material
for this book. Every effort has been made to trace the owners of
copyright material, though in a few cases this has proved impossible
and we apologize to any copyright holders whose rights may have
been unwittingly infringed. We trust that in the event of any
accidental infringement, the owners of the material will contact
us directly.

British Cataloguing-in-Publication Data
A catalogue record for this book is available from the British Library

ISBN 0–281–04961–0

Typeset by Dorwyn Ltd, Rowlands Castle, Hants
Printed by Biddles Ltd, Guildford and King's Lynn

Contents

❧

This book sprung to life as a result of seeds sown in lunchtime discussions with members of The Wednesday Group and so it is dedicated to my friends in this group – with my gratitude for the space and time each has given so that, together, we could safely wrestle with perplexities and paradoxes and debate freely with one another in a confidential, accepting, understanding and non-judgemental atmosphere.

—— 1 ——

&.

Good Enough for God

Our chance to be healed comes when the waters of our own life are disturbed.

(Elizabeth O'Connor in Kelsey, 1986)

On the face of it our aims and our desires often seem simple enough – 'I want to live a fulfilling life!', 'I want to be happy and contented', 'I want to be free to serve God as I think he wants me to', 'I want to find a partner, to have children and enough money make life satisfying', 'I want work', 'I want a home', 'Above all, I want to be fit and healthy'. But, when it comes to seeking to fulfil our expectations, many of us find that we are limited less by insufficient support from outside ourselves and more by the poverty of our inner resources. At times, we may glimpse how limited we are in ourselves, and how our woundedness cripples us.

THE SEARCH FOR HEALING

In one of his poems, 'Healing', D. H. Lawrence painted a telling verbal picture, portraying what had gone wrong inside himself when he became ill. Within his picture's frame, he showed how illness assumed significance and he discovered it to be a source of rich meaning and of new life. He was clear that his illness involved more than him being simply some kind of human mechanism which had started to malfunction. 'I am ill,' he explained, 'because of wounds to the soul, to the deep emotional self.' He then went on to share from personal experience that the healing of such wounding not only takes a very long time, but also requires 'a certain difficult repentance', a 'realization of life's mistake' and 'the freeing oneself from the endless repetition of the mistake' (Lawrence, 1964).

In my experience, most (if not all) of us are suffering in one way or another. Life has wounded us from infancy onwards and we still bear the emotional marks and scars of our hurts. In some cases, these are invisible; in other cases they are all too apparent. Some of us have looked in the direction of religion, hoping that through faith we would find the deep kind of healing our souls so need. We *may* have found what we sought, and in Jesus Christ, the wounded healer, our hurts have been taken away. On the other hand, we may have been disappointed in our simple trust that faith, and faith alone, would heal us. Many of us require deep healing of our inner-most selves, similar to that mentioned in D. H. Lawrence's poem. This often requires skilled understanding, as well as the expenditure of time, endless patience and (unless we can find help for free) financial resources, in order to appreciate and deal with what it is that has hurt our inner selves so deeply.

Others of us fail to realize how wounded we are, and how crippled is our emotional self. We show the world our 'coping self'. We may even manage to deceive ourselves to such an extent that the outer mask becomes the only part of ourselves with which we are familiar and on good terms. We reveal only our outer self, wearing a beautifully embroidered, bejewelled cope that covers the vulnerable, secret self that is clad only in sack cloth and smeared with the ashes of that of which we are so ashamed. Should anyone sniff our secret (that somewhere around our person is a distressed, neglected baby self whose nappy desperately needs changing) we feel we would die of shame. And so we limp through life, disguising our lopsided-ness and disability until such a time as things go so wrong that our bodies or our minds let us down in a catastrophic way.

We may then find ourselves both turning towards God and searching for emotional healing. This is not necessarily the destructive catastrophe we assume it to be. It may signal the crisis of birth rather than death. Such physical or mental breakdown may have the salutary effect of making us stop to take stock of ourselves. We can no longer blindly and mind-lessly plod along, nor, blinkered, charge headlong through life; we are forced to pause and ponder. Our bodies or minds refuse to work as they used to, so we have no choice but to rest; we are forced to be quiet. We may feel we are drowning in overwhelming mental flood waters, or slowly dying of star-vation and neglect in the isolation of intense inner loneliness, or sense a terrifying empty nothingness, as if we are dead and entombed, like a Lazarus bound, stinking, in a shroud but with not a hope in heaven or hell of resurrection.

In our pausing, and in our prayers and meditation at such a time, we may be unable to escape the horror of our inner bankruptcy. We may be unable to pray or to think, and our very inertia and immobility communicate more than words or thoughts could ever articulate. We have come to the end of our rope. We may sense that we must now find the divine or die. In our anguish, either in words or in our silence, we cry out to God for healing. Our agony seems unbearable. And it is at this point, for some of us, that we turn in the direction which leads us towards inner rebirth. We have reached one of those transforming moments in life in which (we later realize) our healing was dependent on our ability to loosen our grip on some of the things we once held dear. As Jesus said, before we can find life, we first must lose it. Our illness, then, con-tains the potential to become, for us, a 'healing illness'. We understand what Elizabeth O'Connor means when she writes that 'our chance to be healed comes when the waters of our own life are disturbed' (in Kelsey, 1986). Our plight forces us to seek meaning relating to ourselves, meaning that escapes our attention while life is free of pain or intense discomfort.

WHERE THAT SEARCH MIGHT LEAD US

Some Christians wriggle and squirm at the thought that it might be necessary, or even desirable, to seek meaning and healing for emotional wounds from sources outside the walls of their church. 'Only Christians can safely bring healing to Christians!' is, in some places, an unwritten, firmly held

belief. That well-trained, responsible counsellors or thera-
pists who may have a different religious orientation could be
as effective in facilitating the resolution of inner wounds as is
any qualified surgeon of integrity to suture outer wounds is
deemed suspect in such circles. Fear of the unknown breeds
suspicion. In some people's minds, that which is unknown
and outside the safety of the familiar church fellowship is
assumed to be also outside God's loving sphere of influence
and so must be avoided. Some Christians then thoughtlessly
churn out phrases along the lines of 'Freud ranks next to
Lucifer!' or 'Let a psychotherapist loose in your brain and you
let in the devil himself' or 'If you want to keep your faith then
faithfully resist any influences from those outside the Church
– especially those adept at bending minds'. Taken to an extreme (which I caricature to make my point) the choice may
appear to be a stark one: 'Either make sure your eternal salvation is watertight or risk your spiritual welfare by allowing an
unbeliever to dabble with your soul!'

I believe that, by and large, psychotherapy and counselling
from well-trained professionals is complementary to Christianity, not in competition with it. I have seen that it is possible and fruitful for the practitioners of each to respect and
value the other, and for the two to move and work hand in
hand. For instance, a senior Jungian analyst writes, 'The
purpose of Jung's argument was not to put psychology in
place of religion but to use the insights of psychology to see
religious truths more clearly. Jung valued religious experience, which offers people an irrational experience of their
inner selves which psychology could deepen' (Astor and
Fordham, 1995). Religious understanding may be regarded as
speculation, something that cannot completely be proved,
but is, none the less, valuable and valid. Another Jungian
analyst explains that, as he sees it, 'Religion depends upon
faith in the transcendental reality of God, and rests upon a
kind of reality which transcends every experience. Religion,
in particular theology, looks at the phenomena from their
metaphysical position, and comes to conclusions about the
nature of God; psychology looks at them from the theory of

the collective unconscious and comes to conclusions about human nature' (Fordham, 1958). Jung believed that religion (which comes from the word *religere*, to reflect) is one of man's basic instincts, it is a natural need that must, therefore, be satisfied.

TALKING SEMANTICS

Part of the misunderstanding that may arise between the religious person and the one speaking from a psychological perspective seems to be due to linguistic confusion. In commenting on the differences between theologians and psychologists, Jung points out that 'both appear to speak the same language, but this language calls up in their minds two totally different fields of associations. Both can apparently use the same concept and are then bound to acknowledge, to their amazement, that they are speaking of two different things' (Jung, 1969). When this happens it is not surprising to find the one misinterpreting the other.

I think that this confusion is inevitable at times as both the theologian and the psychologist are concerned with profound matters. Both move beyond the sphere of conscious awareness and into that of the unconscious. The unconscious is deeply mysterious – it is only partly known – and is terrifying to many people. It has been said to be 'God-like in its awesomeness'.

I am intrigued to discover that, at heart, psychoanalysis shares some crucial ideas with Christianity. Some aspects of what is important to the one are also important to the other. A dictionary definition of the word 'analyse' is 'to examine in detail in order to discover meaning, essential features, etc.' (*Collins English Dictionary*, 1988). Analysis involves reducing a complicated thing to its simple or primary elements. The Greek word from which it is derived means 'to undo, to unbind, to unloose, and to set at liberty'. The verb and its cognates were used in classical and biblical Greek to refer to setting out on a journey, whether by striking a tent or casting off from moorings. Interestingly, the story of a psychological analysis is usually the story of the undoing of that which was tightly bound, and involves setting out on a perilous journey, during which the person concerned comes to discover something precious within. Equally, when someone comes to Christ, he or she sets out on a journey during which great risks are run but great riches are uncovered. Along the way, hopefully, chains are loosened and the Christian experiences the great liberty available in Jesus Christ. In both cases, healing comes about through an ever increasing experience of wholeness.

We are told in the Bible that we should 'work out your own salvation with fear and trembling'. The word 'salvation' carries within it meanings relating to 'wholeness' and 'healing'. This is something many of us have to work at – on our own or accompanied by someone else. We may fear starting off on such a journey, but can find strength and courage by understanding that 'it is God that worketh in you'.

The paediatrician and analyst Donald Winnicott coined the phrase the 'good enough mother'. He pointed out that what babies and children need more than anything else is a mother who is 'good enough'. She does not have to be perfect – perfection anyway being beyond the reach of ordinary mothers. In the same way, it is my understanding that God wants us to be children who are 'good enough' for him. He does not expect some kind of perfection that is beyond our reach but, rather, wants us to try to become the kind of disciples who, in the original Greek meaning of the word 'perfect', are whole, healed and complete people.

MY JOURNEY

As I took time out to think about these matters, I found myself on a fascinating journey of discovery and understanding. I share some of my findings with you in this book. However, my journey has still thousands of mental and emotional miles to go. It is as yet incomplete – I have not arrived – but, as I suspect I never shall end this journey, what I have to share are fragments of thought. Take them if you will, digest them, see whether they offer you nourishment and food for further thought yourself – food, after all, is necessary for our growth.

2

A Perplexing Project

> If only I could just figure out how I really feel, as opposed to
> how I think I'm supposed to feel.
>
> (Anonymous)

The time is past, in a high proportion of modern church
cultures, when Christians are handed a tidy package of beliefs at the moment of 'conversion' and told to 'hold fast to
the faith of the fathers' and 'not to doubt, for doubt is of the
devil'. However, this is still not always so, as I discovered
the day I met Mandy.

MANDY'S DOUBTS

Fresh out of her evangelical Bible college, she bounced up
the stairs to our flat, flopped down on the couch, accepting
the mug of coffee I knew to be essential to a student's sur-
vival, and the two of us talked non-stop for the next couple of
hours. A torrent of words tumbled out of Mandy, punctuated
every ten minutes by a swig of coffee and relieved comments
like, 'I didn't know that there was any other Christian anywhere who'd not only understand how I felt, but also who
wouldn't nag and tell me that it was a thoroughly bad thing to
be spilling over with so many questions and doubts . . . and
who wouldn't tell me I ought to gird up my loins of faith and
keep on believing regardless.'

MY DOUBTS

I warmed to Mandy. She was honestly expressing the kinds of
thoughts that I had buried, unexplored, inside myself when I

was her age and which had only surfaced, like exploding landmines, in mid-life. By that time I was a missionary, serving with the type of missionary society for whom the kind of doubting Thomas I had become since I had been taken on by them was an embarrassment (to me and I suspect to them also, although they were too kind ever so say so). I envied Mandy's ability to question. It meant that she would not have to struggle later on with the long-term effects and the resulting problems and inner wounds of repressed and denied problems, such as those traumatically forced to my attention in my mid-thirties. I had lived the first half of my life not really questioning a certain set of Christian assumptions that were wrapped up in a neat belief package until the time when the questions refused to stay lying down quietly any longer. Then, painfully and unwillingly, I was forced to grapple with them through the kind of faith crisis and life crisis that had led me to a desperate cry for help and a suicide attempt fifteen years before I talked with Mandy.

I had believed it when I had been told by senior Christians whom I looked up to that 'doubting is sin'. I had struggled for years to work up enough faith to be able to accept that all those things I was taught were essential beliefs for 'real Christians'. 'Real Christians' were those people who were 'born again Christians' or 'Bible-believing Christians' (as opposed to the other sort whose faith the likes of me were arrogant enough to deem to be 'suspect'). As far as I was concerned, doubting was extremely dangerous. It was better to ignore problems than to admit their existence and try to face them.

I was sharing my story with Mandy, as well as listening to hers, and telling her how terrible it had been when my Christian world fell apart and it seemed as if I had lost God because I could no longer believe everything I used to accept so trustingly. I shared the terror I had experienced lest my questioning implied that I was on an extremely slippery slope leading away from faith. Our eyes met and I knew she understood. Then I added, 'But I didn't realize that I had been given the gift of doubt!' Mandy nearly dropped her coffee mug. She was startled by the expression 'the gift of doubt'. A grin slowly spread across her face and her eyes sparkled as she said, 'Just tell that to any of my Christian friends – they'd never believe you'd said it . . . doubt a gift . . . you've got to be joking!'

THE GIFT OF DOUBT

I explained how, as a teenager, when I had become a Christian, I had been given 'the gift of faith' but then, later in life, the 'gift of doubt' had been thrust into my hands and seemed like a most unwelcome present. Mandy beamed, 'I like it . . . the gift of doubt'. I liked it too.

For years I had missed the meaning of the words 'doubt is the workshop of faith'. I had deemed such words to be nonsense – for doubt and faith could not rub together creatively as far as my understanding went. I assumed that doubt would automatically destroy faith. However, in the years following my crisis of faith, loss of certainties and the discovery that life is more complicated than I had previously assumed it to be, I discovered that God is far more mysterious, greater and deeper, more distant and intimate, more knowable and, at the same time, more unfathomable, more loveable and hateable than I had previously thought.

I also took the plunge and did something I would have previously thought too risky: I studied theology and then psychology. To my amazement, I discovered that, far from my faith shrivelling up and shrinking into nothingness when seen through both theological and psychological microscopes and telescopes, my struggles to make sense for myself of Christianity turned my faith into something far plumper, sweeter, stronger and richer than anything I had known before. At the same time, paradoxically, faith was something that, at times, seemed more skimpy, unedifying, fragile, bitter and poverty stricken than it had been in the past. My Christian uncertainty had been transformed into a certainty that I now had a faith in which there was room for uncertainty. Our time was up and Mandy rose, saying, 'Thank you for showing me that I can be real. I can be true to what I think and feel and know that it's possible for faith to be enriched and not ruined through questioning and doubting' (*Woman Alive*, 1994).

I was beginning to develop the capacity for what John Keats calls 'negative capability'. He explains that this state exists when 'a man is capable of being in uncertainties, mysteries, doubts, without any irritable reaching after fact and reason' (Gittings, 1968). This way of approaching life is very different to the reasoned, scientific manner that I grew up with. The state of negative capability is worrying at times, uncomfortable and stressful. I like to feel safe, knowing that I understand those things I need to understand; I like to feel confident that I know about God. This way I feel as if I have greater control over what may or may not happen. Having control is something someone with a personality like mine values highly. When I am in a position of leadership, as long as I do not overdo it, others value my ability to steer things safely, but when I am in another role, my need for control can be a handicap. So, developing a capacity to live with uncertainty left me anxious and worried, until I grew more accustomed to this way of being and discovered that, at times, it could also be exhilarating and exciting. Not being in control of certain things is not only possible for me but, I found, does not lead to the disaster I sometimes assumed it would do. Contrary to expectations, my faith did not fade away into nothingness in the face of my uncertainties. I had always assumed that I had been called to live 'the life of faith', but I began to appreciate that life for a faithful Christian believer could also contain an extremely valuable component of disbelief, as expressed in the words 'Lord, I believe, help thou mine unbelief' (Mark 9.24).

I began to tussle with other ways of gaining knowledge that began to make sense to me and which proved to be unexplored ways in which understanding was given when the rational let me down. For instance, the doctor and psychoanalyst W. Bion suggested something that made little sense to me until I began playing with his idea in my mind and found it to contain an illuminating idea. He wrote, 'Instead of trying to bring a brilliant, intelligent, knowledgeable light to bear on obscure problems, I suggest we bring a diminution of the "light" – a penetrating beam of darkness; a reciprocal of the searchlight.' There was something about his apparently crazy, back-to-front suggestion that increasingly made sense to the 'me' who had spent most of her life trying to bring the bright light of logic into dark places. He goes on to explain that 'the darkness would be so absolute that it would achieve a luminous, absolute vacuum. So that, if any object existed, however faint, it would show up very clearly. Thus, a very faint light would become visible in maximum conditions of darkness' (Bion, 1974).

CHALLENGING IMAGES OF GOD AND OURSELVES

I began to explore worlds outside the one that had been bounded by the safety of a certain prescribed set of beliefs. Studying theology and psychology in the 1990s opened my eyes to the work of Christians and non-Christians whose ideas and thought patterns were quite different from those in which my evangelical roots lay. In particular, I found it a great relief to try to 'figure out how I really feel, as opposed to how I think I'm supposed to feel', as the words of a card I saw framed on the wall in a psychotherapist's loo put it. It was painfully and exasperatingly true, as it also said on the card, that 'deep thinking screws up another perfectly nice day', but, despite the discomfort, it was something I found to be infinitely worth trying.

In particular, I was forced to notice that one of my treasured concepts – that of God being a nice, kind, all-powerful daddy who would look after me, as long as I was his good little girl – was being tested. Psychology challenged me to dare to listen to Sigmund Freud, and other analysts who followed him, and to start to grapple with some of his arguments, which was extremely uncomfortable. Freud argues that the image people have of God is generally formed and structured by their childhood experiences of their own father and by

their adult need for a father figure (Freud, 1953). I did not
want to hear this! I suspected that if I began to explore
Freud's ideas in any depth, I might discover that what he said
contained elements of truth and that it might be disconcertingly true that I wanted to find a father in God. This left me
anxious. I was afraid that, should it prove to be true, my
cherished beliefs about an all-powerful Creator God, who was
completely kind, all-knowing and all-loving, would then melt
away. My erstwhile fundamentalist certainty squirmed at
being tossed about in this way. I also realized that, at times, I
might want to find a mother in God. I did not know what to
make of that.

However, events in my shaking outer and inner worlds
meant that I was forced to consider these uncomfortable concepts, and also to try to understand those internal processes
termed psychological 'defence mechanisms' (Freud, 1968). I
struggled to try to understand how this might fit in with my
set of religious beliefs. It was very confusing at first. The
more I began to see what I was really like on the inside of
myself, the more I came across aspects of myself I did not like
at all. There were certain sides to me that I kept as secret as I
possibly could – often not allowing even myself access to
these hidden parts of myself. Having begun to notice the
reality of these dark aspects of myself, I began to discover
more about some of the contents of my secret inner world. I
became aware that, in common with other people, I adopted a
useful mechanism to dispose of some aspects of myself I did
not want. This is called 'projection' by psychologists. It involves attributing feelings inside myself of which I dis-
approve to another person (Campbell, 1987). By this handy,
deceptive mechanism, I manage not to be in touch with feeling my own, disliked and shameful aggression. I put it elsewhere and thus can say of the unsmiling greengrocer, 'Look
how hostile he is to me – he never gives me the best fruit.'
His grim face suggests to me that inside him is a psychic hook
waiting, ready for me use to hang some of my own unwanted,
shameful, despised feelings on without my being aware of
what is happening. I project some of these feelings into him

and thus remain blind to some of the contents of a part of my inner world with which I prefer not to be familiar. In this way, he can be the hostile one and I can be the nice, kind, unruffled one. That suits and supports an image of myself I like to maintain. I can remain in blissful ignorance about the angry, destructive streak running through me, failing to realize that I see in him something that is really part of myself.

I discovered, to my initial consternation, that a whole load of feelings that were unacceptable to me and filled me with shame (like aggression, anger, hatred, jealousy, envy, destructiveness, certain sexual stirrings, to name but a few of those feelings I would prefer not to have) had been bundled up and distributed, like letters posted through letterboxes and delivered, to people I liked as well as those I did not like. I managed, completely unconsciously and unaware that this process was going on, to project many of these feelings into other people so that they carried them for me.

I now clearly understood words from sermons that had annoyed me in the past and said, in effect, 'If you point one finger at another person, then there are three fingers pointing back at you yourself.' I was uncomfortably reminded how Jesus taught that we should be more concerned about removing the beams or planks from our own eyes and less preoccupied with the motes or tiny specks in our brothers' eyes (Matthew 7.1–5). I began to notice that if there was something I saw in another person that I disliked intensely, then it was salutary to examine myself to see whether there was anything of that detested quality in me. I found I had a sneaky habit, in common with other people, of unconsciously splitting off things about myself that I could not accept and of projecting those qualities right out from myself and into someone else.

This psychological defence mechanism also works in a back-to-front manner, so that, at other times, we may find that we regard another person as being everything we have wanted to be and feel, which we now somehow manage to convince ourselves that we are not. This is contrary to objective reality about ourselves. In this way our acceptable qualities can also be projected away from ourselves (Coate,

1989). This mechanism may occur when a group of Christians see their leader as being all-caring and all-understanding and themselves as inadequate and sinful.

If, unconsciously, we have problems with being the object of another person's envy, then, without knowing we are doing this, we may invest that other person with some of our enviable qualities. We then feel incompetent or lacking in knowledge, and this is preferable to living in a state of unease, not knowing if or when we will come under fire from the other person's envious attacks. On occasion, this is mistakenly referred to as 'Christian humility'. It may appear that someone is truly humble when, in reality, but unconsciously, they are dead scared of being envied and try their hardest to avoid it. Someone who was envied as a child by one or both parents is particularly vulnerable to this. When this defence mechanism is at work, it is not possible to comply with the biblical injunction 'I bid every one of you not to think of himself more highly than he ought to think, but to think with sober judgement' (Romans 12.3).

The defence mechanism of projection can work in yet another very powerful way at times when we are really desperate. It may be that for us to connect with strong feelings of anger seems intolerable. We may, without realizing it, be fearful that our anger might tear us apart or completely overwhelm and drown us. At these times it may not be enough for us to look at another person and see them as furious or whatever. We can, quite unconsciously, try to project our unacknowledged anger into the other person and, further, get him or her to behave angrily towards us. We may then feel attacked and persecuted by something we see as *outside* us that, in fact, originated *inside* us. The name given to this sort of process is 'projective identification'. So far, so good, but there are times when this actually works at an even deeper level so that 'the person responding to us sometimes actually feels what we need them to feel and then does react accordingly; when this happens we call it *introjective identification*. If their reaction is very unlike how they usually feel or act they may be able to twig that something odd is happening and begin to resolve it. If it is rather nearer the bone for them then the situation may go on escalating unchecked' (Coate, 1989). When we, or others, act completely out of character, then it is possible that projective identification is powerfully at work within us.

I suspect that, at times, some Christians unconsciously use this mechanism and find that they are being 'persecuted for the faith'. Could it be, unlikely as it seems on the face of it, that some get mocked or scorned for their faith while, all the time, the catalyst for this has unwittingly come from within themselves? This kind of thing is difficult for us to unravel and to understand because superficial inspection of ourselves is likely lead us to react with the words 'What nonsense!' However, greater understanding and increasing self-awareness may reveal that a hidden part of ourselves is needing to be 'persecuted' or punished, possibly so that temporarily we feel a little less guilty about something of which we are probably completely unaware. This kind of increasing understanding comes when we painstakingly peel different layers off our inner selves, like stripping the layers off an onion one by one.

I suspect that some of us who tend to find that no matter where our work takes us, we seem to land in some kind of 'trouble' because of our beliefs, may inadvertently and unknowingly have set things up so that this happens to us. We may even manage to gain extra spiritual brownie points when our fate is prayed for in the church prayer meeting; we are praised as being 'heroic', and put on a little pedestal as an example to be emulated, as someone who nobly suffers and endures for their faith. We may feel even more satisfied – in a perverse kind of way – should it be added that we suffer as Christ suffered, for now we are identified with the divine. This subtle or blatant kind of Christian martyrdom may well be suspect and may not be what it appears at face value. However, we have a problem as all this is happening at an unconscious level of our minds and so we are unaware of what may be going on and, therefore, have no choice in the matter. We have to drift along, caught up in the current of what is happening.

WHERE DOES THIS LEAVE US?

This may seem fairly straightforward, but, once I started to explore how projections and our attitudes to God may be intertwined or merged or confused or misunderstood, I found the matter less easy to grasp and tidily pigeon-hole in my mind. Freud suggested that God should be got rid of. He declared that God was invented so that those who childishly needed, among other things, some kind of fathering, could try to obtain feelings of being parented by God. His solution was that people should grow up!

I find that I do not need to take the radical step of dispensing with God completely. I would suggest that we have been created with the unconscious ability to use our inbuilt psychological mechanisms to try to make up for and cancel out inner deficiencies and deprivations and that this may be very useful for us. Some of us may unconsciously attempt to do this, with varying degrees of success, by finding in God something we need and did not receive in adequate supply in childhood or infancy. I see this as an acceptable use of our inner resources. Some of us may have a degree of awareness of what we are doing and see why we do it. Others may simply get on with it and find satisfaction in the way they relate to God. Freud might call it running away from reality, but I see this as a human and acceptable way in which some of us cope with living with ourselves. Different people find different ways of dealing with inner needs, psychic wounds, anxiety and inner conflict.

What I find unacceptable is some Christian teaching that implies or states clearly that all of us, all of the time, have to be exactly like one another. The message goes like this: 'Our way is God's way and there is no other way of coming to God.' This is then backed up by a selection of verses from Scripture to prove whatever point is being made. Any biblical teaching that hints at other possibilities is ignored. Some of us, some of the time, may have similar belief patterns to one another and act from similar surface motives, but I believe that we are misled when we arrogantly insist that everyone else in the world must be as we are if they are to find God's salvation and get to heaven. I find it extremely presumptive to add the 'God factor' to this and to claim that 'everyone must be like us because we are what God intends all people to be'. Sadly, some of us, Christians, do just this. Needing other people to be as we are, people who mirror us by their beliefs, preferences and actions is, in adults, a mark of a particular form of psychological damage inflicted on a person in infancy. It is a sign of the narcissism from which we all suffer to a greater or lesser extent.

It is held by many thinkers that personally and collectively we form images of the God we worship and to whom we pray that are 'fashioned out of what we need and what we wish for. Our pictures of God come from the memories of a real experience of dependency on our parents and their responses to us. They come from our own fantasies about our parents' responses, in which we endow them with better or worse actions than they performed. Our pictures of God come from longings still within us, as for a strong ally who will protect and comfort us' (Ulanov, 1985). It is also suggested that we form an internal picture of God as being someone who is able to help us deal with aspects of ourselves that cause us difficulty. We are back to another way in which we unconsciously may use the defence mechanism of projection. This can come about as a 'result of impulses we cannot accept in ourselves – usually of aggression and anger – that we delegate to this surrogate champion. We need someone larger than life who understands us and our fears. We want a God who will guarantee that life will be fair in the end, that the wicked will be punished and the good rewarded. Above all, we need an intermediary with the unknown. Our various pictures of God make this possible' (Ulanov, 1985). Bible stories are a rich source of illustrations of the manner in which God has been used to bring solutions to human dilemmas, and used to try to give meaning to some of life's happenings that otherwise appear senseless.

There are times when I need to find in God a special quality of fathering and I find it acceptable to use God and

my feelings about God in this way. The Bible suggests that
God has no objections! There I read words like 'you have
received the spirit of sonship. When we cry "Abba! Father!"
it is the Spirit himself bearing witness with our spirit that we
are children of God' (Romans 8.15) and 'As a father pities his
children, so the Lord pities those who fear him' (Psalm
103.13). I can experience God as the father I need at times
and enjoy the feelings of safety at being fathered that this
engenders. I can also simultaneously hold in my mind my
understandings about the mechanism of projection.

At other times, I need to find in God a special quality of
mothering and take comfort in words like 'you shall suck, you
shall be carried on her hip, and dandled upon her knees. As
one whom his mother comforts, I will comfort you' (Isaiah
66.12, 13) and 'How often I would have gathered your children together as a hen gathers her brood under her wings'
(Matthew 23.37). Whether the feelings aroused in me of
being mothered by God have been produced by the mechanism of projection or not, it is still an important part of my
religious self to be able, at times, to experience God as a
comforting parent. If Freud objects to this, then I respond
with 'That's tough! It's something I need at times and can't
get from anywhere else. It enables me to get through and so
I'm not giving it up!'

It appears that some of my friends feel the same as me.
Within six hours of writing these words, I received three
greetings cards, all expressing the universal longing to be
close to the great and good mother. Anna's card was a Pre-
Raphaelite painting *Night and Her Train of Stars*. Gentle,
beautiful mother night swept across the skies, her wings
forming a womb-like enclosure in which nestled a train of
baby angels, and cradled in her arms was the tiniest of the
baby angels. Her finger on her pursed lips was saying to the
others, 'Ssh! Don't wake this special little one.' Anna said
shyly, 'I want to be like that baby angel.' Berthe gave me a
card showing a mother penguin gazing with love at a bedrag-
gled baby penguin curled up contentedly at her feet. I remembered how she had told me that a mother penguin walks

hundreds of miles across ice and snow to find her lost baby. Berthe has always wanted a mother like that. Julie's card was a photograph of a very young child leaning safely in the cradled palm of a giant hand. Its fingers curved around the child, the child's eyes closed in sleep. Julie often took comfort in imagining that God cared for her like this. Her card bore words written by Mother Julian of Norwich: 'In His love He wraps and holds us. He enfolds us for love and He will never let us go.'

3

Underlying Blueprints

The living image of the great and good mother has at all times of distress been the refuge of humanity and ever shall be; for the state of being contained in the whole, without responsibility or effort, with no doubts and no division of the world into two, is paradisal, and can never again be realized in its pristine happy-go-luckiness in adult life.

(Neumann, 1989)

SUSAN'S EXPERIENCE

Susan's face was unusually soft and gentle when she tried to explain what she had experienced at church the previous Sunday. I was intrigued as she was usually tense and anxious when we met, and tended to be upset and angry about one thing or another. Today she seemed different.

She told me that she recently listened to someone preaching who had experienced God in an unusual manner when on holiday in Toronto and wanted to share what had happened to him with people in Susan's church. She listened, at first with boredom but then attentively with unusual and growing interest, beginning to be drawn to this man and the things he was sharing. He seemed to be talking about something bigger than himself or his own personal experiences. At the end of the sermon, anyone who wanted to 'give themselves to God afresh and to receive the new thing the Holy Spirit was waiting to give' was invited 'to walk to the front of the church for special prayer and laying on of hands'. Susan found herself moving forwards. Then the quietly enthusiastic preacher stood by her, his hands trembling, arms raised and almost flapping like wings over her head. She could hear a few other people laughing and moaning, as if with intense pleasure. Then, suddenly, she collapsed and slumped to the floor. Her fall did not hurt her. She lay, along with others to whom something similar had happened, for about half an hour, experiencing what she described as 'complete bliss . . . like floating around supported by warm water in the Dead Sea. . . . I wasn't worried about anything. God was holding me close in his arms, like a really wonderful and loving person, but he didn't want anything from me – he was there to give me everything I needed. I've never known anything like it'.

The effect of that experience has remained with Susan and I am glad about this. As a child, she had known next to no love from her mother. As an adult, few had really cared for her. The chip on her shoulder and her difficulty in relating to others could easily be explained by her past. It seemed to me that Susan, while she lay relaxed on the floor, had experienced God as being like an amazingly good mother to her. The way in which she talked reminded me of a baby in the womb or of a contented baby at the breast enjoying abundant supplies of rich milk. She agreed with me when I shared my thoughts with her. Indeed, the expression on Susan's face reminded me of that of a baby who has a full and comfortable tummy, experiencing 'baby bliss' with not a care in the world.

I could grasp some aspects of what might be going on inside her, both in religious and psychological terms. I was reminded of teachings given hundreds of years ago by the Christian mystic Saint John of the Cross. He wrote, 'It must be known that the soul, after it has been definitely converted to the service of God, is, as a rule, spiritually nurtured and caressed by God, even as is the tender child by its loving mother, who warms it with the heat of her bosom, and nurtures it with sweet milk and soft and pleasant food, and carries it and caresses it in her arms' (Saint John of the Cross in Fordham, 1958). Something similar is hinted at in the Bible, in the Epistle of Peter: 'Like newborn babes, long for the pure spiritual milk, that by it you may grow up to salvation; for you have tasted the kindness of the Lord' (1 Peter 2.2, 3).

Susan's experience reminded me of something other people in other situations have described, which could be referred to as an experience of what has been called 'the great and good mother archetype'. Psychoanalyst Erich Neumann explains it like this: 'The living image of the great and good mother has at all times of distress been the refuge of humanity and ever shall be; for the state of being contained in the whole, without responsibility or effort, with no doubts and no division of the world into two, is paradisal, and can never again be realized in its pristine happy-go-luckiness in adult life' (Neumann, 1989). Stories of the experiences of Christians down the ages have often included their account of their encounter with the God who holds and contains them in a safe embrace, as a mother cradles a much-loved infant.

CHERRY'S EXPERIENCE

When Cherry told me what had happened to her in a similar meeting to the one Susan went to, she shared an experience that was very different to Sally's, of God being like an experienced and caring mother. Cherry's experience involved a terrible sense of abandonment, emptiness and fear. She remembers repeatedly screaming 'No, no, no!' at the top of her voice, while trying to extricate herself from disturbing feelings that threatened to drown, overwhelm and destroy her. She finally returned to her normal state of mind but felt as if she was dead. The effects of this lasted many months, leaving her distraught.

RECONCILING SUSAN'S AND CHERRY'S EXPERIENCES

I find that I can make some kind of sense of this by postulating that Cherry encountered the opposite side of things that Susan experienced. I think it likely that Cherry connected with the archetypal 'great and evil mother'. Susan encountered the positive pole of the archetype, and Cherry the negative. Some of her church leaders told Cherry that what had happened to her was caused by a Satanic attack and they prayed vigorously that the evil spirits harming her would depart from her. Their prayers, however, did not change her feelings and she did not lose her prolonged sense of horror and fear at what had happened to her.

I find the wording of her leaders' diagnosis – 'Satanic' – unhelpful. For me, the possible explanation that this is due to a frightening encounter with the negative pole of the maternal archetype is more satisfying. Cherry, through work with a psychotherapist, is now also encountering the positive pole of the archetype. This seems to have come about through her sense that her therapist is like the good mother she lacked in childhood. Her relationship with God is shifting gradually and she is beginning to experience God as kind and loving again. If experiences like Susan's and Cherry's may be attributed to experiencing an archetype, then we need to understand a little more about archetypes.

WHAT ARE ARCHETYPES?

The word 'archetype' is an ancient one, deriving from Platonic writings which proposed that there were ideas in the minds of the gods that served as models for human beings. The word archetype has been defined as being 'one of the inherited mental images postulated by Jung' (*Collins English Dictionary*, 1988). According to Jung, 'Archetypes are typical modes of apprehension, and whenever we meet with uniform and regularly recurring modes of apprehension we are dealing with an archetype, no matter whether its mythological character is recognized or not' (Jung, 1978). It can be imagined to be like an original blueprint, something usually laid down in the minds of all peoples, of all races and in all times. An archetype has been likened to an empty jug within the psyche waiting to be filled. It is a potentiality available for realization in the right circumstances.

Archetypes of different kinds exist within the international collective unconscious of the human race and move into the personal unconscious of every individual. In trying to describe this, Jung talked of the existence of an imaginary three-layered internal structure within each person. It was composed of surface conscious awareness, under which rested the layer of personal unconscious (this is unique to each individual) and, deepest of all, lay the impersonal or collective unconsciousness (which was universal).

In his efforts to make sense of what was happening both in his own inner worlds and those of his patients, Jung imagined that, in the deeper layers of the unconscious, there existed (in the words of a later analytical psychologist, James Astor) 'nodal points around which experience and emotion gathered, such that they acquired characteristics which he described in terms of the images that these nodal points gave rise to. He called these structures archetypes, and the images archetypal images. The images are not inherited but Jung postulated that there was an inherited predisposition to form images' (Astor and Fordham, 1995). Thus, today, we might illustrate this by pointing to research into how we learn language, which indicates that, up to puberty, 'human beings are "hardwired" to produce syntactic structures, but each person learns their own language' (Astor and Fordham, 1995).

A variety of archetypal images exist, like those of the divine child, wise old man, hero, trickster, wounded healer and the god image. The 'god image', in Jungian terminology, is also equated with the archetype of the 'self', and part of its function is to carry out an unconscious process by which healing and integration proceeds in one's inner world. Jung's use of the word 'self' carries different meanings in different places in his writings and at different times in his life and, therefore, a concise definition of it cannot be given here.

Another way of trying to understand archetypes can be gleaned from the writings of the modern analyst Rosemary Gordon. She explains that, according to Jung, 'the physical expression of an archetype takes the form of instinctual activity, and its mental expression the form of images. He has also compared them to the invisible presence of the crystal lattice in a saturated solution. The archetypes, so Jung makes clear, are devoid of content to begin with until personal experience renders them visible and hence potentially conscious. They may also be thought of as psychic "programmers"' (Gordon, 1978). Thus, archetypes are manifest in the way in which people behave, especially at times of basic universal human experiences such as birth, death, separation, marriage and motherhood. They have their counterpart in people's inner psychic lives, and are experienced in various ways, such as in dreams, fantasies and experiences of God. They also present as patterns of behaviour.

I find this way of thinking, and this kind of a model, helpful in relation to the experiences of Susan and Cherry. Jung regarded archetypal images as conscious representations of that which also exists in the unconscious, which is made up 'both of instinct and of spirit. Thus an archetypal image has a bipolar quality, reflecting the way energy in the psyche travelled between opposite poles. According to Jung, integration of the opposites was the task of the second half of life when the struggles of the ego had been achieved' (Gordon, 1978). Archetypes, then, hold in tension two extremes at opposite poles. A dictionary of Jungian thought suggests that 'an infant tends to organize his experiences of early vulnerability and dependence upon his mother round positive and negative poles' (Samuels, Shorter and Plaut, 1992). Jung himself states that the positive pole draws together such qualities as 'maternal solicitude and sympathy; the magical authority of the female; the wisdom and spiritual exaltation that transcend reason; any helpful instinct or impulse; all that is benign, all that cherishes and sustains, that fosters growth and fertility' (Jung, 1992). In short, the good mother. The negative pole suggests the bad mother: 'anything secret, hidden, dark, the abyss, the world of the dead, anything that devours, seduces, and poisons, that is terrifying and inescapable like fate' (Jung, 1992). It is, however, important for us to realize that 'Jung's theory of archetypes led him to hypothesize that the influences which a mother exerts on her children do not necessarily derive from the mother as a person and her actual character traits. In addition, there are qualities which the mother seems to possess but which, in fact, spring from the archetypal structures surrounding "mother" and are projected on to her by the child' (Samuels, Shorter and Plaut, 1992).

THE NUMINOUS

Something dramatic and extraordinary had obviously happened to both Susan and Cherry. Each powerfully sensed the presence of something, someone, which was hard to describe in mere language. Another quality about an encounter with the archetypal is the strange intensity of the encounter and the sense of something occurring that is clearly out of the ordinary. It is here that I find parallels with my own religious, theological and psychological ways of understanding. Such an encounter is referred to as an experience of the 'numinous'. The 'numinosum' is described by Jung as 'a dynamic agency or effect not caused by an arbitrary act of will. On the contrary, it seizes and controls the human subject, who is always its victim rather than its creator. The numinosum – whatever its cause may be – is an experience of the subject independent of his will . . . the numinosum is either a quality belonging to a visible object or the influence of an invisible presence that causes a peculiar alteration of consciousness' (Jung, 1969). This is familiar to me. I know of people experiencing the feeling of being seized and controlled by something greater than themselves. When this is benign, then a Christian is likely to attribute this to God or to 'being filled with the Holy Spirit'. The opposite feeling is often attributed by certain Christian groups to 'the devil'.

Such an encounter is impossible to explain away, for the person involved is an impressive witness to its validity. It is obvious that something remarkable has taken place in that person. An encounter with the numinous has the characteristic of conveying an individual message that, though mysterious and enigmatic, is also deeply impressive. These experiences cannot be forced on a person against his or her will for, at some level, conscious or unconscious, a person must be ready to trust a transcendent power before he or she can experience that which is numinous. We cannot, by an effort of will, *make* ourselves experience the numinous; all we can do is open ourselves to it. Should it then become ours, it is likely that it will 'happen upon us' with tremendous and compelling force, and will hold an important, attractive, but initially undisclosed, meaning. We sense that something amazing has happened, but we may not know what is implied by our own experience. Such understanding of the meaning of the experience tends to come later.

THE ARCHETYPAL AND THE NUMINOUS

There are two ways of viewing that which is archetypal. One perspective focuses on the working out of certain archetypes, and the other on the archetypal within a person's deepest being, within his or her psychic self. Jung describes the simultaneous instinctual and spiritual character of the archetype and says that the 'term is not meant to denote an inherited idea but rather an inherited mode of psychic functioning' (Jung in Harding, 1955). He suggests that this corresponds to 'the inborn *way* according to which the chick emerges from the egg; the bird builds its nest; a certain kind of wasp stings the motor ganglion of the caterpillar; and eels find their way to the Bermudas'. He points out that 'it is a pattern of behaviour' and says that 'this aspect of the archetype is the biological one – it is the concern of scientific psychology'. However, he makes it clear that 'the picture changes at once when looked at from the inside, that is from within the realm of the subjective psyche. Here the archetype presents itself as numinous, that is, it appears as an experience of fundamental importance. Whenever it clothes itself with adequate symbols, which is not always the case, it takes hold of an individual in a startling way, creating a condition of "being deeply moved", the consequences of which may be immeasurable' (Jung in Harding, 1955). The study of profound religious experiences convinced Jung that at times of such experiences, previously unconscious mental contents break through the ego boundaries. They move out of the unconscious and overwhelm the conscious personality. This is similar to the way in which the unconscious sometimes invades consciousness in psychological illnesses. In this particular case, of course, the person is not actually ill. Contemporary humanistic psychology refers to such impressive religious experiences as 'peak experiences'. If you are a Christian who experienced conversion to Christ as a sudden, intense experience that dramatically changed you, then you may well find echoes of your experience of God in these thoughts about the archetypal and the numinous.

Paul seems to have had such an experience on the Damascus road when he was hurled to the ground by God's blinding light. Throughout the Bible, encounters with God often take the form of being something awesome and out of the ordinary. Such encounters are often transforming. Jungian analyst Joseph Redfearn speaks of religious experience from his psychological perspective and says that 'one aspect of the overwhelming power of God is clearly the overwhelming of normal consciousness by virtue of excess of experience. Indeed direct and unfiltered exposure to God is commonly felt to be lethal, or necessarily so, and this is why it is sometimes supposed that he is understood or creatively experienced, only through indirect means – symbols, signs, portents, intermediaries, messengers, representatives, and similar attenuated forces' (Redfearn, 1992). I am reminded of Moses and the burning bush, of Jacob wrestling with the man who turned out to be none less than God, and of the stranger who walked with the disciples on the road to Emmaus. Redfearn goes on to write about his patients' experiences of God, which were usually conveyed to him in terms of God being found to be 'comforting, reassuring and as a kind person by nature . . . In dreams . . . when someone called "God" appears, it is usually a surprisingly ordinary person, a grandfatherly figure, or an administrator for example' (Redfearn, 1992). This leads him to suggest that 'it could mean that our notion of God – not merely intellectually but at depth – is of a basically simple and childlike sort' (Redfearn, 1992). We are back on familiar territory – that of our tendency to project unwanted aspects of ourselves into others. Redfearn points out that when this happens, the 'dark, terrible aspects of reality and of our deep selves are split off from the personal and are projected, as it were, on to images of nature and impersonal physical forces . . . it might mean that . . . we are simply not at present capable of assuming personal responsibility for the more destructive feelings and wishes in ourselves' (Redfearn, 1992).

Conversion, Pentecostal and charismatic experiences, being 'filled with the Holy Spirit', and experiencing the Toronto blessing suggest to me that here people may well be experiencing what analytical psychologists refer to as the God archetype or the Self archetype in numinous intensity. I agree with another Jungian analyst, Nathan Schwartz-Salant, who observes that 'the numinous strikes a person with awe, wonder and joy, but may also evoke fear, terror and total disorientation. Being confronted with the power of the Self arouses just such emotions, which always and everywhere have been associated with religious experience'. (Bear in mind that in Jungian analysis, the archetypes for Self and for God are the same.)

Nathan Schwartz-Salant goes on to describe how in his clinical experience some of the reactions of fear, or awe, are common to people seeking an encounter with the living God. He says that 'there are at least three major forms that fear of the numinous quality of the Self may take. First, there is the fear of being flooded with archetypal energies and of being overtaken by a will greater than that of one's ego' (Schwartz-Salant, 1982). His words express the fearful longing experienced by many Christians, who deliberately consecrate themselves to God and then wait for the Holy Spirit to flood their beings. 'Being filled with the Spirit' and being as overwhelmed as the early Christians were on the day of Pentecost is described in terms of being drunk and of being possessed by a benign power and energy over and above that which is human. It is something for which many Christians simultaneously long and fear.

'Secondly,' Schwartz-Salant observes, is the possibility that 'the fear of the Self and its energies stems from an abandonment fear. Over and over again, I have met the following attitude, "If I contact all that strength and effectiveness, no one will be able to be with me, I'll be too powerful and everyone will send me away"' (Schwartz-Salant, 1982). For some Christians, connecting with the Holy Spirit's fullness has meant ostracism. Exuberant, 'Spirit-filled' Christians are out of place in many plodding, quieter church cultures, and such Christians tend to migrate to places of worship that are home to others like themselves. To be the only 'tongue-speaking', 'singing in the Spirit' Christian in a church fellowship can be an isolating and lonely experience. Envy takes root and camps form composed of the haves and the have nots.

This links with the final point made by Swartz-Salant, who suggests that 'closely related is the fear of taking hold of the energies of the Self because they can be so appealing and beautiful that one is certain he will become the object of envy. He will sacrifice and hide the Self to avoid envy's "evil eye" . . . The person terrified of envy . . . acts very much like this, only a bit worse: he also hides his prize from himself' (Schwartz-Salant, 1982). The Christian who has experienced the Holy Spirit in a profoundly moving way often tends to keep silent about what has happened – intuitive fear of the unconscious envious attacks of others shuts his mouth. Were he or she to speak, his or her precious experiences might be spoiled by the words of others. Words of Jesus may be taken as relevant and seem to encourage such silence: 'Do not throw your pearls before swine, lest they trample them underfoot and turn to attack you' (Matthew 7.6).

As I was thinking about Susan, I remembered that her mother had always envied her daughter and had managed to spoil and wreck her achievements in one way or another. Unconscious fear of being envied has been built into Susan's inner self. I am not surprised, therefore, to see the way in which she now plays down the experience she had of God as a loving nurturing good mother with everyone she contacts. Within months she had even managed to convince herself that nothing much had happened to her. I think that, at times, expressions of so-called Christian humility may have their roots in the unconscious fear of other people's envy rather than being a genuine Christian virtue.

To discover that one way of thinking about God can be in terms of Jungian archetypes and the numinous does not in any way negate or diminish the greatness or the reality of the God I worship. It offers me a useful model through which my finite mind can make some kind of sense, satisfying to me at present, of the infinite. It is not my only way of seeking to know God, but it offers me a useful tool, for which I am often grateful.

4

❧

Rooted in Infancy

> Our need for others has its roots in our earliest experiences
> and is bound up with our deepest feelings.
>
> *(Josephine Klein, 1987)*

CHILDHOOD'S INFLUENCE ON THE ADULT

Built into each of us is a tendency to repeat our earlier patterns of being, of feeling or getting rid of unwanted feelings
and reacting. These repeated tendencies are often similar in
some way to how things were in childhood. Usually we are
unaware that this is happening, but it is intriguing, and dis-
arming, once we are conscious that we may be doing this, to
notice certain repeating patterns in our lives. We may see this
in certain occurrences in our personal situations or in what
goes on inside or around us. Some things may have a vaguely
familiar ring to them. We may sense that we have been in a
past situation that is similar to the present one. Whether we
like it or not, we bring the effects of the factors that shaped us
as children into our adult Christian lives and it is salutary to
explore this as much as we are able to. This takes different
forms and has various twists and turns in individuals' lives. It
is illuminating and life-enhancing to try to be aware of our
personal repeating patterns.

In some church subcultures, the exercising of an attitude of
'complete dependence on God for everything' is often pro-
claimed to be the ideal way in which to live successfully as a
Christian. Bible verses are used to back this up. A favourite is
'He who abides in me, and I in him, he it is that bears much
fruit, for apart from me you can do nothing' (John 15.5). This
is commonly taken with a huge dose of common sense and

the gist of the meaning is taken to be saying something like someone who tries to do the opposite of what is obviously God's will is likely to land in trouble. It is rarely taken to mean that which the words seem to imply at face value. However, there are some people who *do* take these words very literally. They then manage to deduce from these words that anyone who tries to do anything using human initiative, brains, energy and skills is playing on a sticky wicket. They may say something to the effect that 'Unless you do God's work in God's way, you're doomed to certain disaster!'

Sometimes, this is taken a stage further and an implication is drawn that 'God's way' involves taking Bible words like 'I can do all things in him who strengthens me' (Philippians 4.13) and, by turning them upside down and inside out, taking them to mean that 'I therefore *ought* to render myself incapable of using my God-given abilities, so that I do not successfully carry out what I am perfectly able to do'. It seems crazy when stated like this, but those who *do* get on and use their initiative, without first spending hours in prayer asking God whether he really wants them to do whatever it is, may feel that their faith is substandard and if they were better quality Christians they *would* have spent a lot of time asking God for help ahead of time. Some outside observers may gain the impression that such a Christian is trying to perform some kind of self-castration to render himself or herself impotent. 'Whatever is going on?' the observer may ask. It appears, at best, to be folly and, at worst, madness.

Those with such an attitude may even be awarded a shining halo by like-minded people, as the reward due to one who apparently is seen to obey Bible teaching like 'Let him who boasts, boast of the Lord' (2 Corinthians 10.17). It does seem very strange to people outside this kind of church culture that able-bodied Christians should talk as if they were little children, had not yet grown up and wanted to make sure that their heavenly Father knew that his power and authority was unlikely to be challenged by his adult children. In such cases it seems as if the capacity to be infantilized by God and by the Church is turned into a Christian virtue, and that growth into mature adulthood is suspect. It seems even stranger when the person concerned is able to function as a normal competent adult at work but in church life turns himself or herself into someone who is like a dependent child. I think that some of these attitudes, held by very sincere Christians, unwittingly have their roots more in that person's infancy than in justifiable interpretations of Scripture.

THE OEDIPUS COMPLEX

Many other factors were also at work in all of us, shaping us when we were very young, a significant one being referred to as the Oedipus complex. The Oedipus complex is connected with young children's unuttered theories about the birds and bees, storks and gooseberry bushes. Our fertile imaginings about sexual activity all started inside us at an age when we were too small to know anything about sex. It is highly probable that very little children have wonderful fantasy worlds, about which they tell no one for this commences before children have developed clear descriptive powers. In fantasy all kinds of exciting sexual goings on are imagined, accompanied by delicious sexual feelings, plus or minus the unconscious guilt that accompanies the imagining of the getting of forbidden fruit. This may start as far back as the feelings, akin to those of sexual satisfaction, which a baby has as it guzzles at its mother's breast. The development of these sexual feelings and imaginings is a normal but unconscious part of every child's development. The better we worked through our fantasized imaginary relationships as children, and the more satisfactorily we were able to resolve the disparity between what went on inside us and what happened outside us (in our relationships with the real adults around us as children), the less complicated our adult relationships will be. Our earliest sexual stirrings, understandings and misunderstandings influence our unconscious worlds as adults, the way we relate to other people in our outer worlds and, at times, the way in which we relate to God, like a father or mother.

Legend has it that, despite his intentions to avoid doing this, Oedipus unknowingly managed to murder his own father and marry his mother. His story is taken to be one that symbolically reflects the inner-world situation common to people in many different parts of the world. Freud was the first person to put forward the theory that children aged between two and five years were sexually interested in the parent of the opposite sex. His studies indicated that it was usual for a little boy to wish to possess his mother completely. This meant he would have to dispose of his father somehow and might wish him dead. However, this simple longing for fusion with his mother conflicted with the love which the little boy had for his father. How could he wish death upon someone he loved so much? A further complicating factor was his disconcerting sense that if father discovered these incestuous and destructive wishes harboured by the lad, then he might respond by turning his back on his son and rejecting him or might punish him physically or, if he were sufficiently angry, might even chop off his son's sexual apparatus. A similar situation exists for little girls – this time, the object of desire being the father. This can, at times, be found in reverse (or 'negative') form so that sometimes little boys long to be possessed by their father and to be rid of their mother, and little girls to merge with their mother and dispose of their father.

It may be hard for some of us to both grasp the theory and accept the probable truth of the Oedipus complex when we first come across it. It may seem impossible for us to imagine something like this. It happened when we were too young to remember clearly what was going on inside us and is at a level of our minds that is unconscious and, therefore, as we are unaware of it, the theory may well seem like a highly improbable and fanciful notion. We may shrug it off, finding the whole theory distasteful and something we would prefer to be without. We are well defended against conscious understanding of certain things about which we prefer to remain in ignorance. However, the experience of many people (both in the world of the arts – great writing, painting, sculpture, music and so on – and in the world of psychological exploration and insight) seems to confirm the validity of this hypothesis.

The ways in which this theory can work out are complicated, with many possible scenarios. Obviously, the incest taboo and the effects should it be violated in reality (as opposed to fantasy) play havoc with childhood Oedipal ideas, complicating matters further. I am intrigued at how Oedipal material from childhood is worked through by some people as adults and in their church life. There are many different ways in which the Oedipal conflict may manifest itself, for church families are usually led by an authoritarian male (often called 'Father'), whom women tend to flatter and try to please and with whom men tend to avoid conflict. It seems also that in *some* instances an attitude of opposition to the ordination of women as priests by men or women *may* also be rooted in unresolved childhood Oedipal conflicts being acted out by the adult.

If you allow your mind to play with the fantasy of the possible consequences of a boy having sexual intercourse with his mother, or a girl having sex with her father, then you will begin to glimpse what is possibly going on at an unconscious level in our minds. In such fantasies, the mother may be envious of the girl for possessing the father and so the mother needs placating and appeasing to divert her destructive envious attacks, or the mother may have been harmed by what the daughter has done and need protecting and healing, and the daughter may feel guilty for what she has done and fearful of the power she possesses that enabled her to seduce her father, and so on.

PSYCHOLOGICAL DEVELOPMENT – SOME THEORIES

And so sexual feelings and Oedipal matters from childhood greatly affect us as adults. Many other factors from infancy have a bearing on our adult lives and outlooks. The well-known analyst and paediatrician Donald Winnicott was someone who understood little children and spent most of his life thinking about the ways in which their developing minds were likely to work. He was fascinated by the developing ideas and thoughts of babies and children. Among other things, he postulated that a tiny baby was quite unable to work out just *what* had come from *where* or *what* belonged *where* or *what* was the possession of *whom*. His work with many mothers and babies led him to suggest that a small baby got hold of the plausible idea that, in response to its hungry demands, it was able to create its very own breast to supply its needs. All it had to do was to notice its pangs of hunger, discomfort, needing to be cuddled and, hey presto, when, at that moment (if it was fortunate), it wished for a breast to make it better, then one magically appeared. When this occurs, the tiny baby, he suggested, understands itself to have been omnipotent enough to be able to conjure up food supplies exactly when it requires them. This is possible because of the closeness of a tiny baby to its mother, the two of them forming a single unit for a while, as if they are merged and one rather than two people. The baby has no idea that it is its mother who is anticipating her baby's needs and who puts the nipple into its mouth just when it needs food and comforting. As far as the baby is concerned, it has worked a special magic to produce this wonderful breast. From the baby's point of view, there is something godlike and wonderfully omnipotent in its ability to do this. Then, as the baby is increasingly able to notice what is going on, hopefully (and usually!) it begins to get hold of the correct idea that its apparent brilliance in being able to produce milk was an illusion. The baby's mother gradually, and carefully, disillusions her child by means of the weaning process and by not popping her nipple into its mouth every time it might like to suck (Winnicott, 1971).

I suspect, that some adult Christians, when in particular need of comfort (perhaps to comfort an inner very young, baby aspect of themselves), may, like me, and without knowing quite how it comes about, experience God as being like a nurturing, caring mother who holds them close to the breast, safe in loving arms. Because we have been created by God with certain sensitive and special psychological mechanisms, these are ready and available to us without our being aware that this is so, and we are able to use them at times of need. This may be one of the ways in which we humans are able to feel very aware of God's comforting presence in the face of despair, loss, anxiety and so on.

As a baby gets a little older, it usually then finds an object outside itself that conjures up feelings similar to those associated with the mother's breast. Technically such an object – a piece of blanket or soft toy – is called a 'transitional object'. Winnicott explains that while it stands for the associations with the mother's breast 'the point of it is not its symbolic value so much as its actuality. Its not being the breast (or the mother), although real, is as important as the fact that it stands for the breast (or mother)' (Winnicott, 1971). He goes on further to explain that the importance of this is that once 'symbolism is employed the infant is already clearly distinguishing between fantasy and fact, between inner objects and external objects, between primary creativity and perception. But the term "transitional object", according to my suggestion, gives room for the process of becoming able to accept difference and similarity' (Winnicott, 1971).

This becomes of more than academic interest to Christians for Winnicott connects the adult use of symbols to an important part of mature religious experience and to the use of symbols in the Church. He suggests that something important occurs in adults in that area of the psyche that in infancy used to be the emotional 'space' existing between mother and baby. It was in this space that the infant first imaginatively played in its inner world and created all kinds of things, like the transitional object that represented its mother but was not its mother. The blanket or toy made it seem to the child as if its mother's breast (or, rather, then, the bundle of emotions associated with it) was there, when external reality made it clear that it was not. To Winnicott, 'it seems that symbolism can be properly studied only in the process of the growth of an individual and that it has at the very best a variable meaning. For instance, if we consider the wafer of the blessed sacrament, which is symbolically the body of Christ . . . for the Roman Catholic community it is the body, and for the Protestant community it is a substitute, a reminder, and is essentially not, in fact, actually the body itself. Yet, in both cases it is a symbol' (Winnicott, 1971).

Our feelings about our mothers and the others in our families have posed a familiar, age-old problem for humanity. That of sibling rivalry was noted by Saint Augustine in his *Confessions*, written as long ago as AD 397. He writes that he has observed jealousy in a baby and that he knew what jealousy meant. He explains that the child in his mind 'was not old enough to talk but, whenever he saw his foster brother at the breast, he would grow pale with envy' (Augustine, 1961). Augustine accurately highlights something else crucial in human development – the sense that a child may have of envy both of the mother's breast itself which is so full of goodness, and also of any sibling or other rival who competes for the goodness supplied by the breast. This idea has been widely explored by psychoanalysts. The mother's breast itself, as well as its contents, leads to feelings of great delight, satisfaction, frustration, love, hatred, tenderness and destructiveness in her children.

I find rich food for thought in some of these ideas. Donald Winnicott first studied under another analyst, Melanie Klein, who was influential in her teachings about the existence and the long-term effects of inborn jealousy and envy. She explores some of the feelings a baby may have and paints a picture of 'child development in which initially the child lives in a simplified world in which people and things are either good or bad (gratifying/frustrating, loved/hated, pleasurable/painful) and never both' (Black, 1987). This state of affairs goes on for a time until the child reaches the stage when it achieves being able to live with 'ambivalence'. This means that the child is now able to 'recognize that it is the same "object" (mother for example) who arouses in him *both* feelings of love (for her milk, her caring etc.) and feelings of hatred (for her absences, limitations etc.). A mature recognition of reality requires the realization that nothing is perfect, and perhaps that nothing is unrelievedly evil. Such a realization makes relationships more difficult, in that feelings now have to be contained and not always acted on, but the difficulty results from a true perception of the world's complexity' (Black, 1987).

Analyst David Black explains that in cases in which 'ambivalence' has not been 'achieved', the result is adults 'whose feelings towards others are a succession of passionate idealizations and raging denigrations, or (more stably) of loving feelings towards one person subtly balanced by hatred towards some other. This leads typically to a sort of Cowboys-and-Indians, us-and-them view of the universe'. He suggests that 'the Christian picture of God and the devil has often been misused to collude with an infantile picture of this sort' (Campbell, 1987).

When I try to get hold of some of these ideas, I find that I begin to appreciate how complicated we human beings are and how certain things in church life and in Christianity that once seemed very clear and simple turn out to be fascinatingly complicated, with different layers of meaning and understanding.

5

&

Grit in the Oyster

Wounded oysters build out of gory wounds a pearl.
And create within the gap of pain a jewel.
May we be so wise.

(Shannon)

JIM'S WORDS

His enthusiasm was infectious and I felt myself getting caught up in the words tumbling out of Jim's twenty-five-year-old mouth: 'Give God everything you've got to give . . . only the best is good enough for him . . . after all, Jesus says that we must be perfect like God is perfect'. I could hear others in the room responding with warm mutterings under their breaths like, 'That's right', 'Yes' and 'Amen to that!' I knew the words from the Bible to which Jim was referring and had heard them often – 'You, therefore, must be perfect, as your heavenly father is perfect' (Matthew 5.48).

ONE INTERPRETATION

As Jim spoke, mental pictures were conjured up in my mind. One of these derived from a children's chorus which exhorts us to 'be a sunbeam for Jesus'. In other words, for Jesus' sake we are to be bright, shining, beautiful and as perfect as a ray of the sun's light. But, at that precise moment, I also remembered that, when my children were teenagers, I had invented a subversive version of this chorus for family consumption only. This was my somewhat scathing, sadly at times all too true, commentary on my impression of the way in which some Christians behave. It was about doormats, and had the refrain, 'a doormat . . . a doormat . . . I'll be a doormat for Jesus!' In a strange kind of way, it seemed to me at times that some Christians equated living as God wanted them to live with lying down and being walked over by all and sundry, and with basking in feeling virtuous as a result. The words I did not use at that time, but which came to me later were words like 'masochistic' and 'self-punitive'.

It took me a long time to realize that not only does God himself rarely, if ever, call us to submit to this kind of treatment, but also that some of us Christians tend to allow it to happen to us for reasons that, possibly, may be connected with some unconscious guilt lurking deep inside that is temporarily relieved if, from time to time, we receive treatment akin to punishment. And we receive this at our own hands, from those of others or as being from God, completely unaware of what is happening. We may experience a sense of things feeling better (we may even feel a mild virtuous glow) when we are treated badly or passed over. We tend not to look at the situation in depth, to explore what might going on and may grab what seems to be a watertight 'spiritual' answer. We may assume that we are experiencing 'the peace of God which passes understanding' because we have some idea that we are being what God wants us to be without stopping to question whether there may be more to it than this. I think that feeling 'peaceful' when we are treated less than well does *indeed* 'pass understanding' for an unconscious process, mobilizing psychological defence mechanisms, may be going on inside us that enables us to get rid of unwanted feelings of resentment and leaves us conscious only of feeling unperturbed. We are left feeling 'peaceful' but, unwittingly, have performed some unconscious mental gymnastics to repress, deny or somehow banish the feelings we prefer not to notice are very much a part of ourselves. We consign them to the unconscious parts of ourselves rather than make them part of our conscious awareness. This may enable us to feel contented but, in the long run, this tendency of ours sows seeds that may spring to troublesome life later on.

STRIVING FOR PERFECTION

Listening to Jim, and knowing a little of his life story, I could see that, true to his youthfulness, he was naturally whole-hearted about anything he was keen on. But, I also wondered whether part of his enthusiasm for 'being perfect for God' was connected with his unnoticed sense of guilt for his own unacceptable, unwanted and disliked feelings buried inside him that were connected with the inadmissible probability that he was not really the kind of son his father had longed for. His father once made this clear by giving his pale, thin, asthmatic son a football and a cricket bat for his eighth birthday – he wanted Jim to play in teams and to succeed as he had. But Jim's body could never cooperate with games – bookworms do not score highly in sports. Jim did not find words to admit, even to himself, how hurt, angry and distressed he really was that his father did not accept him as he was but wanted Jim to be what he could not be. He was not aware how much he wanted to do something to get back at his father and score over him in some way. Instead, Jim excelled in his studies and gained good grades while training to be a doctor, but lurking below the level of conscious awareness was a sense that he was not really good enough for his father, and never could be. I had a hunch that there were times when Jim tried to compensate for this by trying his hardest to be exactly what his *heavenly* Father seemed to want him to be – he was striving to be 'perfect' for God. There seemed to be ways in which his life was directed towards trying his level best to be what male authority figures (father-like men and God) wanted him to be.

FORMING IDEAS OF GOD

Psychologists have put forward ideas as to how children's ideas and beliefs about God are shaped by their experiences with their parents and earliest care-givers. I find some of Sigmund Freud's thinking helpful, even though it led him to conclude that God was a necessity created by those whose psychological development was stunted and so not for mature adults.

Freud put forward his theory about God as it relates to males. He suggested that a little boy formed his image of God on the basis of his experience of his own father. He believed that it was most usual for a little boy to admire and love his father. It would be natural for such a child to regard his father as being the most powerful, kindest and wisest creature in the world. God, for such a child, would be like an overblown and exalted picture of his father. Freud taught that when a boy reached the age of around five or six, he then began to identify himself with his father and see his father as more human and fallible than previously. However, Freud believed that the old exalted image of his father was then transformed into an image of God that persisted into adult life. This means that a young adult who, as a child, experienced their father as being caring and loving, will then have a God they can use as a source of love and as someone who will protect them when necessary.

Freud suggested an adult's relationship with God varied according to their relationship with their natural father or father figure. Such a picture of God is certainly confirmed by many pastoral workers, many of whom would not necessarily agree with the next part of Freud's teaching, which was that, as far as he was concerned, God was a mere relic from childhood and, therefore, God should have no place in mature adult life. As far as he saw it, religion was an illusion determined by wishful thinking. His thesis was that if you want or need a God who is a good, caring, protecting father, then you can *imagine* such a God to meet your desires or your needs.

Despite Freud's atheistic stance, I do find his teaching about God helpful. I often talk with people whose picture of God bears a close resemblance in many ways to the father they knew in childhood, and, at times, to their mother.

Barry and Anne Ulanov explain that, as far as Freud is concerned, there is no God other than the one we create out of our own needs and wishes. There were times when this seemed to be true of Jim. Barry and Anne Ulanov write,

'Unwilling to see that these wishes originate in ourselves, we believe that they come from a being outside ourselves' (Ulanov, 1985). The images of God we have created merely reflect 'our own wishes for consolation against life's harshness. They represent our dread of punishment for the aggression and envy we direct against our neighbour. In short, our images of God personify the unknown we fear. Through them we attempt to control the unknown by turning it into a person like ourselves, only bigger, kinder and wiser' (Ulanov, 1985). God, as portrayed by Jim, seemed to fit into this category.

The Ulanovs point out that God loves us as human beings, all that we are – the physical, intellectual, emotional and spiritual aspects of ourselves. Included in our human nature is the 'psychological process where we take in parts of real people, fashioning from them images of their qualities and our feelings about them' (Ulanov, 1985). We may sometimes place these constructs outside ourselves again and 'then those resultant projections seem quite outside ourselves, as if they had originated far from us and had no existence in us' (Ulanov, 1985). They further suggest that 'we come to God at first through the way we need God to be. Only slowly and with much experience of prayer can we allow God to come to us. Only then, after we have examined and recognized our introjections and projections for what they are, can we really hear another voice than our own' (Ulanov, 1985).

When necessary, we can even use, and misuse, biblical teaching to both back up and cover up from ourselves what is going on. We quote words like: 'Have this mind among yourselves, which is yours in Christ Jesus, who though he was in the form of God, did not count equality with God a thing to be grasped but emptied himself, taking the form of a servant . . . he humbled himself and became obedient unto death, even the death on a cross' (Philippians 2.4-8).

There was something in what Jim was saying that made me realize that the attitude of 'being a doormat' – of submitting to being walked all over, not standing up for yourself and your rights as a human being (and, thereby, without realizing it, denying your intrinsic worth as a person and, by implication, denigrating the one who created you) – was, in some Christian circles, equated with 'becoming more Christlike' and 'moving towards the kind of perfection God longs to see in us'. There were times when I felt sad about the way in which Jim seemed to diminish his personal value and to think that he really was inferior to everyone else. He thinks he is being appropriately humble, but, at times, I see him as donning the ill-fitting coat of a Uriah Heep.

ANOTHER INTERPRETATION AND WHAT IT COULD MEAN

Another picture forms in my mind – that of a perfect pearl, glowing with soft, warm beauty. I had often heard preachers telling me that my life, lived exclusively for God, was to be as perfect as a pearl – an imitation would not suffice. No one seemed to have remembered to warn me (or if they had, I managed to ignore their words) that real pearls are formed in a painful, ugly way. In the words of the poet Richard Shannon, 'Wounded oysters build out of gory wounds a pearl. And create within the gap of pain a jewel. May we be so wise' (Shannon). There is little that looks 'perfect' about an oyster's inner agonized striving and writhing as it tries to rid itself of the sharpness of the irritating foreign body lodged within it. And yet, the horrible woundedness of the oyster contains the potential to form a pearl of the utmost perfection. How can we be perfect while something as nasty as this is going on inside us?

Many of us evade difficult questions like these, we walk away to busy ourselves elsewhere and, in so doing, may deprive ourselves of the pearl for which we long. Yet we cannot escape the fact that, in the biblical narrative, Jesus tells us to be 'perfect'. If we question face-value interpretations of this, like Jim's, how else might we make sense of this passage of Scripture? What do we do about one of the glaring realities of being human, that none of us, not even the most godly, is 'perfect'? I have never met a person who is completely 'perfect', so how is it that Jesus himself tells us to be something that, being brutally honest with ourselves, we know we can never be? Is he sadistically commanding us to be what we cannot attain or is he being unkind in the same sort of way Jim's father was being, letting his son know that something was expected of him that he could never achieve?

Such questions about perfection have exercised Christian minds down the centuries. Augustine of Hippo and the Reformers were clear in their teaching that the goal Christians were to aim for – that of being 'sinless' and thus 'perfect' – was one people were incapable of realizing. They taught that even the best intentions to this end would inevitably be sabotaged by the powerful undermining influence that sin wields in the lives of 'fallen humanity'.

Their words ring true to my experience. For instance, there are times when I am managing to ignore my resentment about something someone has done to me and, on the face of it, am being kind and understanding to that person. I realize later that destructive words seeped out of my mouth sneakily in a casual, apparently harmless comment I make about that person. T. S. Eliot knew about this tendency, lurking, like some kind of undercover agent, within even the best-intentioned of us and expressed it this way:

> Between the idea,
> And the reality,
> Between the motion,
> And the act,
> Falls the Shadow
> (*T. S. Eliot, 1974*)

Struggling with the dilemmas posed by situations like this, other theologians started to explore possible wider definitions of the word 'perfect' and to see whether or not other meanings existed that did not lead inevitably to the conclusion that God asked the impossible of people but, rather, wanted something that it was reasonable to expect. These theologians were looking for a solution that was in harmony, rather than in conflict, with their understanding of God's character, that he is loving, just, fair and, therefore, only makes demands that we can meet. When John Wesley grappled with the problem, his thoughts led him to the conviction that, although people fall short of God's standards, God was not demanding from us the perfection of attaining a state of sinlessness, but, rather, what has been defined as the 'perfect relation of pure love to God, resulting in a life of Christlikeness' (Atkinson and Field, 1995).

PERSONALITY AND OUR RELATIONSHIPS WITH GOD

Undoubtedly, an ideal for which we should strive seems to be put before us by Jesus. This is particularly attractive to those of us whose shaping in childhood makes us respond with a desire (or an unconscious need) not only to live up to ideals ourselves, but also to find other people who live up to the idealized expectations we have of them and who continue to do so. However, others of us, with different factors shaping our adult selves, may be daunted by the thought of trying to live up to ideals. Not only do people fall into several clearly defined personality types that tend to lead them to respond in broadly predictable ways in given situations, but these broad categories are further shaped by childhood nurturing experiences that add further variety to their responses.

Trying to unravel some of this offers a fascinating journey of exploration through unknown territory as we try to discover not only the meaning of the word 'perfect' but also why it might be (apart from our desire to obey Jesus' teaching) that some of us are more attracted towards trying to be perfect while others show no interest in the idea. It is simplistic of those who place a high premium on their own or other's 'perfection' to state derisively of the less concerned ones, 'Of course, they're only second-rate Christians . . . God must have nothing but the best . . .' (the tone of voice being used implying that they are better than these others). It is as if Christians are delivered to heaven pleasingly, quickly and efficiently provided that the envelopes in which they are enclosed bear first-class stamps. Those stamped second class will get there in the end but will be delayed and are less recommendable than those arriving by the perfect route. Certain Christian jargon refers approvingly to the first-class ones as 'having more jewels in their crowns' than the second-class ones, who apparently scrape home to heaven wearing threadbare cloaks and are devoid of coronets.

Several ways of viewing and of assessing personality types have developed from the ideas of Carl Jung, a well-known one, popular in some church circles, being the Myers-Briggs Personality Indicator. After Carl Jung and Sigmund Freud painfully disagreed and separated, Jung reflected on what might have happened to cause such a breach between them, for the men had been close to one another for some time and Jung himself had been like a son and heir-designate to Freud. Jung concluded that part of their inability to see eye to eye, or, rather, heart to heart, arose from their different manner of perceiving and responding to the world. One of them was an extrovert and the other an introvert. Jung began to realize that he could identify four 'functions', or modes, we use to handle the people and problems in our lives. He defines these functions as being 'sensation', 'thinking', 'feeling' and 'intuition'. Different functions are developed to different degrees in different people and we automatically use our strongest functions. He uses a metaphor to explain this. A lion strikes out at its enemy or its prey with its powerful front paw, it does not attack by lashing out with its tail whereas a crocodile does. He points out that, in a similar way, 'our habitual reactions are normally characterized by the application of our most trustworthy and efficient function; it is an expression of our strength . . . an intelligent man will make his adaptation to the world through his intelligence and not in the manner of sixth-rate pugilist, even though now and then in a fit of rage he may make use of his fists. In the struggle for existence and adaptation everyone instinctively uses his most developed function' (Jung, 1989).

Jung's observations of human nature enabled him to see that while some people perceived the world around them primarily through sense impressions, which he called 'sensation', others picked up what was happening 'via the unconscious', which he called 'intuition'. 'Intuition' is paired with 'sensation' as belonging to the so-called 'perceptive function'. The intuitive person is not too bothered about the facts themselves – they seem so obvious that they hold little interest. It is the facts behind the facts, possible hidden meanings, that intrigue the intuitive person. On the other hand, someone of the sensation type will 'take everything as it comes, experience things as they are, no more and no less; no imagination plays around his experiences, no thought attempts to look deeper into them or explore their mysteries – a spade is a spade; neither is any real valuation made; what counts is the strength and pleasure of the sensation' (Fordham, 1953).

In a tangled situation or in an argument where the facts may not lead to a reasoned solution, sometimes it is the inspired guess of the intuitive person that will produce an unexpectedly effective way forward, in a manner that no amount of reasoning could do. To the person working unconsciously according to the strong function of sensation, all this speculation appears to be complete nonsense, and it comes as a surprise to look back and observe with hindsight that another person came to an appropriate end-solution to a problem by, to them, an apparently daft process. My friend Maggie and I often laugh at this – we are opposites (mirror images of each other) in terms of personality type. We have found over the years that, in the end, we come to similar conclusions but by such totally different routes that we laugh and say, 'We've done it again!' Our recognition of this difference in approach yet similarity of results has deepened our trust in each other's conclusions and actions.

As Jung thought further about all of this, he noticed that while some people assess their perceptions through an analytical process, some others do so by assigning value to their perceptions. In his terminology (which is used specifically with this meaning and not that which we give the words in more everyday speech), the former group of people use 'thinking' and the latter group use 'feeling' functions. This pair of functions is called the 'rational or judging function', which comprises 'thinking and feeling'. Taking Jung's meanings for these words, the rational function specifically refers only to the acknowledgement of value, as in 'I feel *this is right*'. In a nutshell, 'thinking judges opinions and statements as true or false, feeling judges people, things or ideas as good or bad, attractive or unattractive' (Bryant, 1984).

These pairs of functions are present in everyone – one of each pair playing a dominant role in each individual, the other a minor role most of the time. A person who is introverted and in whom the functions of intuition, feeling and perception are dominant will have inner and outer processes that differ from those of an extroverted, thinking, sensory and judgemental personality type. So, it is often a waste of time trying to talk in 'feeling' language to a 'thinking' type, and, equally, logical argument may be wasted if it is used to try to convince a 'feeling' type that something is very important. Because, according to Jung, we all have both pairs of all the opposites within us, 'feelers' are still able to 'think', and vice versa, but it is easier to 'do what comes naturally'.

OTHER SHAPING FACTORS

Setting store on living up to certain standards and ideals, and facing difficulty in tolerating those who are less bothered about this, characterizes one of the combinations of these possible different inner factors. People of different personality types view life differently, so, some people will want to be 'perfect' more than others because of their personality make-up. However, the desire to be perfect, live up to ideals and have certain role models who are perceived as ideal people is characteristic of people who have been shaped in childhood by the nurturing they did (or did not receive) in another way. Jim, who we met earlier in this chapter, is a case in point. It is highly likely that his father's longings for a son who was good at football had a hand in shaping Jim's enthusiasm about being 'perfect for God'.

There is more to it than this alone, however. A particular kind of wounding may have arisen in some people that,

among other things, means the child (and later the child within the vulnerable adult) facing life's harsh realities develops a
need, first of all, to find deep understanding, empathy and
'"mirroring" from care-givers; secondly, to form an idealizing
component, which seeks a powerful and good figure whom
the child can admire and in whose glory and perfection the
child can bask. In the first position it is as if the child says, "I
am perfect"; in the second position the child says, "You are
perfect and I am part of you". The availability of these figures
who can either be responsively mirroring of the child's greatness or can carry the child's idealism is crucial to a child's
sense of well-being' (Molon, 1993). We find emotionally
wounded adults in our churches who have an unconscious
compulsion and need for being able to feel that they are
'perfect' and for being seen to be like this. They also may
have an unconscious need to be part of a church fellowship
that seems to be the ideal one or to be attached to a certain
Christian leader of whom they can feel 'You're perfect and
I'm part of you'.

Sometimes parents can give vulnerable children what they
need, but, at other times (due to no fault of their own), they
are not able to do this adequately. If these needs are thwarted
too much or if the child is let down traumatically in some way
by the parent, then the normal compensatory development
does not occur. What should happen is a process in which
'those components of the personality are gradually modified,
through repeated non-traumatic contact with reality and
transformed into mature ambitions and ideals' (Molon, 1993).
Sadly, there are times when this does not take place, and then
'the infantile grandiosity and needs to idealize remain repressed and unintegrated' (Molon, 1993). It is confusing but
helpful to bear in mind, therefore, that the motive to obey
Christ and to seek to be 'perfect' may have several strands
running through it – one of which is an inherent and unconscious need to repair or live with childhood trauma and to be,
find and uphold the ideal at all costs.

When Christian heroes and heroines (those people some of
us blindly follow and almost worship, assuming them to be

infallible in teaching and life) topple off their pedestals and display their messy humanity, this can wound some of us deeply. We, rightly, are concerned lest God and the Church have been discredited, but there may be more to it than this alone. What has happened (to those of us vulnerable in this way) is that we have unconsciously *needed* these idealized people to meet our inner deficits and to be 'perfect' for this reason. Thus, the crashing fall under the glare of media publicity, for instance, of an 'evangelical Pope' or one of his 'cardinals' from the pristine state in which they were idealized and revered into the mire in which the grimy, smelly side of their humanity is all too apparent can be more than just disconcerting. It may seem to some of us as if concentrated sulphuric acid has been poured over a sensitive, hidden wound at the centre of our beings. We react with extreme and over-the-top disappointment to their imperfections and may be furious and saddened by the way in which we seem to have been let down.

Our disappointment may well be like a rope composed of many strands – one of which may be this need of ours to have idealized and perfect people around us. People are created and then shaped to be gloriously diverse. I find this wonderfully intriguing. I am fascinated to discover that as Christians struggle with the task of trying to understand what it means to 'be perfect', factors other than logic and pure reason are going to play a strategic part.

6

The Perfect Fit

> I do not say to thee, 'Seek the way',
> for the Way itself has come to thee.
> Arise and walk!
>
> *(St Augustine)*

LUCK AND 'THE PLAN'

'It could be you!' booms the seductive voice from the television set, as a supernatural luminous hand descends with outstretched forefinger, penetrating my sitting room and pointing straight at me. 'Wow!' I would exclaim, leaping to my feet and unable to believe my luck, if it *were* me and if I had been lucky enough to come up with all the right numbers to win several million pounds for the small investment of £1.00 in a national lottery ticket.

My delight would last all of three seconds, though, for the voices of my inner Mafia would promptly move into their fun-spoiling accusatory mode and start clamouring, 'It *shouldn't* be you, you *shouldn't* gamble like this . . . you should follow God's plan for your life, not have anything to do with luck . . . you should only have money you have earned by working and doing what God wants you to do – gambling is bad and if you gamble then you're bad . . . *you* are bad.'

Then I might recall the occasion when, casually wanting to wish well to a friend as she went out of the door for a job interview, I shouted 'Good luck!' It was as if I'd hurled abuse at her. She turned on her heels to face me, reprimanding me with the words 'How could *you* possibly say that? We're both Christians and we don't believe in luck – we believe in God! If it's God's plan for me to get the job, then I *will* get it.' I felt just two feet tall.

Within seconds of winning, I expect that I would then find myself feeling familiarly guilty for not really succeeding in following 'the plan'. This 'plan' was, someone told me when I was a teenager, that which God had organized in his mind, before the world was created, especially for me to follow. I was told that it was imperative for me to follow it for many reasons. Among them was the so-called 'fact' (or could it have been fiction?) that if I failed to play my part, doing what God wanted of me, then that detailed part assigned to me in his plans for the whole world would go awry (like a tiny defective cog marring the workings of a giant clock). God would then have to find another way of doing things without me, which, of course, he could usually manage to do but it would be a nuisance for him. On those occasions when God, for some unspecified reason, was unable to find a substitute for me, then, I was warned, his plans would have to be cancelled and I would have let him down very badly.

This idea was sometimes reinforced by a quotation from the Bible, 'Teach me thy way, O Lord, that I might walk in thy truth' (Psalm 86.11). This was taken to imply that there was one way of truth, and only one way, in which Christians were to walk in obedience to God. Alternatively, a frightening verse might be used like, 'Son of man, speak to your people . . . if the watchman sees . . . and does not blow the trumpet, so that the people are not warned . . . his blood will I require at the watchman's hand' (Ezekiel 33.2, 6). To be held responsible for the damnation of another human being was awesome. It was a good stick with which anyone could beat the donkey-me into action, and into exerting maximum effort to try to 'save' everyone I came into contact with, as well as the entire world by giving money to missionaries and evangelists. Then, hopefully, I might escape punishment from this God who, it seemed, was out to get me if I failed to do exactly what he wanted. In the first half of my life, I did my best to understand and to follow whatever it was that seemed to be God's plan for me, but the older I grow, the harder it is to see what precisely this plan might be. If an exact tailor-made plan for my life does exist, then I am not sure I have managed to follow it very well so far.

SNAKES AND LADDERS

I used to think that it was as if my Christian life contained a number of ladders I could climb up. But one, and one only, was the ladder God had *planned* for me to ascend, to get nearer to him, and, in the end, arrive in heaven to hear his 'Well, done, good and faithful servant – you have followed my plan for your life.' I had a hunch that, unless I was extremely careful, I could end up on the *wrong* ladder and climb to a place God had *not* planned for me or that a 'wrong ladder' could turn into something like a snake and I would slide down and across the black and white squares of the board game of life, never reaching my heavenly goal. If I indulged in sinful things, such as playing games of chance like the lottery, then one of the rungs of my ladder would fracture, even break completely, and I would tumble to the ground.

The black and white ground rules of my childhood and teens were clear and full of shoulds and shouldn'ts. My parents and grandparents taught me that the church raffle belonged in a forbidden 'bad' black square and so, without doubt, the national lottery belongs in forbidden territory. I was supposed, if I needed to touch the ground, to walk only on the white squares of 'following God's will and becoming perfect'. Life appeared amazingly and unrealistically sanitized viewed from such a bleached perspective.

LIVING WITH THE MAFIA

Should I do the forbidden and land on a black square, then the chairman of my 'internal Mafia', an elderly fatherly man I called the 'evangelical Pope', would state censoriously that he was praying for me as I was so obviously trying to run my life as *I* wanted to rather than following in God's way. I was then doomed to ruin. How, I imagined he would ask me, could I 'walk in God's way' if I got myself money by such dubious means – money that might give me access to places and to things that were not part of God's plan for me? Such a lifestyle would forfeit God's blessing. Obviously, I am over-stating my case. I have used raffles and lotteries as an extreme example of the kind of process that goes on inside some of us church people. This process, though, can be set in motion regarding all kinds of activities and thoughts.

It is now a number of years since I recognized the power that my Mafia-like conscience has within me. As well as the chairman, there are members of my secret inner organization who resemble the authoritarian, judgemental, male figures of my past. I am increasingly aware of the confused and untrue words with which (with my consent) they used to run rough-shod over my life – words that none the less sounded biblical, plausible, pious and Christian. They talked a great deal about how I must 'please God', 'honour God', 'serve God' and 'bow down to God'. It did not occur to me to question them. There were times when it did not enter my head that God might be other than a very powerful ruler who must be placated and obeyed. That it might be possible for God to be ruler, king, lover, mother, creator and destroyer had not occurred to me. The watchword, frequently sung or said, was that 'Jesus is Lord!' The implication drawn from this was that immediate obedience, like that of slave to master, was expected. I had yet to realize that areas of mutuality and complementarity could exist between God and people, mirroring the relation-ship between the three different Persons contained within the Godhead.

For many years of my Christian life, I had assumed that as I was in a state of 'born again-ness', I, therefore, had 'arrived'. I knew Jesus' words: 'Unless one is born of water and the Spirit, he cannot enter the Kingdom of God . . . whoever believes in him should not perish but have everlasting life' (John 3.5, 15). My assumption was that, having 'believed and been saved' (Acts 16.31) at my conversion, at 9.15 pm one Saturday night in August at Eastbourne Town Hall when I was fourteen years old, I had met the requirements and was now 'saved' and belonged to 'the Kingdom' (Acts 16.31). My illusion was that everything was now all right, and the only thing I had to do now was (in the words of the popular chorus we sang often) to 'trust and obey, for there's no other way, to be happy in Jesus, but to trust and obey!' However, I gradually and disconcertingly discovered in the years that followed that I did not really understand *how* to 'trust and obey' or what precisely it was that was being required of me by God.

WHAT DOES 'PERFECT' MEAN?

So, if life is not a game of spiritual snakes and ladders, with the goal being that of finding and following God's exact plan for that life, what are we here for and what should we be aiming at?

For me, one answer to this question lies in the word 'perfect', which is translated from the New Testament Greek word *teleios*. William Barclay writes about the use of this word and Jesus' words to his followers – 'You therefore must be perfect, as your heavenly Father is perfect' (Matthew 5.48) – saying, 'on the face of it that sounds like a commandment, which cannot possibly have anything to do with us. There is none of us who would even faintly connect ourselves with perfection'. Barclay then explores the word further and explains that 'the word *teleios* is often used in Greek in a special way. It has nothing to do with what we might call abstract, philosophical, metaphysical perfection. A victim which is fit for sacrifice to God, that is a victim which is without blemish, is *teleios*. A man who has reached his full-grown stature is *teleios* in contradistinction to a half-grown lad. A student who has reached mature knowledge of his subject is *teleios*, as opposed to a learner who is just beginning and who as yet has no grasp of things' (Barclay, 1978).

I am reminded of my time in Thailand, where I worked for fifteen years, and my discovering the uses of the word 'ripe'. Not only was this word used to mean fruit that was ready to eat, it was also used colloquially to refer to a young man who was mature enough and complete enough to have followed the traditional practice for all young men after puberty – entering the Buddhist priesthood for a prescribed number of months. 'He's ripe!' therefore meant that he was now mature or complete and had served his time in the priesthood. 'He's not ripe yet!' meant that something was still incomplete about him, for he had not yet met the prerequisite of being a mature Thai man. I think this fits with William Barclay's explanation that 'the Greek idea of perfection is functional. A thing is perfect when it fully realizes the purpose for which it was planned, and designed, and made'. He adds that '*teleios* is the adjective formed from the noun *telos*. *Telos* means an end, a purpose, an aim, a goal. A thing is *teleios* if it realizes the purpose for which it was planned; a man is perfect if he realizes the purpose for which he was created' (Barclay, 1978).

He finds an apt example of this meaning in the everyday situation of needing to fix a loose screw and trying to find exactly the right screwdriver to do this. On occasion, he realizes 'that the screwdriver exactly fits the grip of my hand – it is neither too loose nor too tight, too rough nor too smooth. I lay the screwdriver on the slot of the screw and I find that it exactly fits. I then turn the screw and the screw is fixed'. Then, 'especially in the New Testament sense, that screwdriver is *teleios*, because it exactly fulfilled the purpose for which I desired and bought it. So then a man will be *teleios* if he fulfils the purpose for which he was created' (Barclay, 1978).

Jesus' teaching that his disciples are to be 'perfect' seems to have caused problems for his apostle Luke. His way round it, when he wrote the part of his gospel that parallels Matthew's similar account, was to put slightly different words into the mouth of Jesus. He has Jesus saying 'Be *merciful*, even as your Father is *merciful*' (Luke 6.36). It is near enough, but not quite near enough, to free us from our problem of what to do with perfection.

Donald Guthrie suggests that 'there are no good reasons why both should not have had some basis in Jesus' thought. But even if we must choose between them, it is by no means certain that Matthew's form must be rejected. No one would deny that perfection is a more difficult ideal than showing mercy. It is unconvincing to suppose that either Matthew or some community created so hard a saying. If we accept its authentic character, we are bound to see in it an aim to bring the purpose of God for man to its final fulfilment' (Guthrie, 1981).

Guthrie agrees that 'the word used (*teleios*) strictly means complete' and then moves our thinking one step further forward by looking carefully at the context in which this particular teaching of Jesus' was given. This teaching comes in the Beatitudes and follows Jesus' amazing statements about the quality of love he longs to see in his followers – a love that enables people to give love in return for hatred, and prayer in return for persecution (Matthew 5.3–48). Such love, surely, can only be a faint reflection of the perfect love of God. He reminds us that 'this saying appears in a context which speaks about love, and it is possible that the perfection in mind is primarily the perfection of love. Perfection is characteristic of the character of God. It should be noted that the only other occasion when Jesus spoke of perfection was to the young ruler (Matthew 19.21) when he told him that in order to be perfect 'he must sell all his possessions and give to the poor where the meaning of "perfect" seems to be "complete"'' (Guthrie, 1981).

WHAT DOES THIS MEAN FOR US?

We face a paradox. We are told to do certain things that we *cannot* do, but we are told to do them as if there is no problem about this and they are possible for us. Further, we are told to expect things in return that we are rarely able to receive in concrete terms in this life, but they are things we might well be able to receive symbolically. Obviously 'the meek' rarely, probably never, concretely 'inherit the earth', nor do the 'merciful' always 'receive mercy', but there are inner, symbolic ways in which the meek and merciful may receive these things. There is also a certain ebb and flow of the tide of opposing feelings deep within our unconscious selves when opposites are brought together and meekness is then fused with its opposite (the quality with which a powerful ruler is imbued) in life's internal crucible.

There are also other indications in the gospels that seem to make it clear that an ideal is set before us which is impossible, unattainable and will be achieved not in the here and now of current living, but in a future then and there, which at times seems to refer to the afterlife. Thus, some biblical interpreters teach that the rewards to be given – the 'blessedness' to be attained by those who succeed in trying to follow the teaching of Jesus in the Sermon on the Mount – will occur in the very distant future. Jesus' commands about the quality of love to be offered have a daunting, unattainable 'all or nothing' ring to them. How, I wonder, can I possibly love God with *all* of myself or even consider that I might manage to love another person as I love myself (Mark 12.29-31)? And yet there is within me, and others, something greater than myself that is drawn to such an over-the-top demand for the apparently impossible and unobtainable.

When this 'over the topness' catches me, I sometimes sense that I may be connected with something greater than my individual self – something that has the power and the universality of an archetype. Something greater than myself has been sparked and connected with. This is something for which it is hard to find words; it defies language. Sometimes I can make sense of it by clothing it in psychoanalytical language. Jungian thinkers postulate the existence within everyone of 'an archetypal urge to coordinate, relativise and mediate the tension of the opposites. By way of the self, one is confronted with the polarity of good and evil; human and divine. Interaction requires exercise of the maximum human freedom in the face of life's seemingly inconsistent demands; the sole and final arbiter being the discovery of meaning' (Samuels, Shorter and Plaut, 1992). Donald Guthrie, whose viewpoint is that of a conservative evangelical theologian, is reassuring when he claims that no one 'who considers himself to have attained perfection already has a right understanding of perfection. Neither is anyone who claims to have arrived at a state of complete love likely to have done so' (Guthrie, 1981).

I find it helpful here to try to further bring together theological and psychological insights and start to think along lines like ones suggesting that 'where Jung spoke of *indi-viduation*, Jesus spoke of *love*. Both were thinking of the fullness of living to which we are all called. Both saw this vocation in terms of likeness to God. For Christians, to be like God is to love, for *God is love* . . . The transforming vision of God, in which we see God as God truly is, as unlimited love, is what brings the created and redeeming image of God to its full flowering in love . . . Jung can help us here to understand the gospel more fully, and the gospel in turn can throw a unique light on the journey toward the integration of personality' (Grant, Thompson and Clarke, 1983).

And this brings me back again to William Barclay's way of looking at this. He claims that 'a man will be *teleios* if he fulfils the purpose for which he was created . . . man was created to be like God (Barclay, 1978). And God's characteristic is that of universal benevolence, unconquerable goodwill, constant seeking of the highest good of every man. .. to love saint and sinner alike. It is when a man reproduces in his life the unwearied, forgiving, sacrificial benevolence of God that he becomes like God, and is therefore perfect in the New Testament sense. The man who cares the most for men is the most perfect man' (Barclay, 1978).

'Perfection' is, for me, summed up helpfully by Francis Wright Beare: 'The charge to be perfect as God is perfect is to be understood as a summing up of all that has been said under the heading "love your enemies". The perfection meant in this context is the completeness of love – a love which is not measured and limited by the character of those with whom we have to do, but is poured out in keeping with the love of God' (Wright Beare, 1981).

Such thinking leads me to conclude that finding my way in the Christian life has nothing to do with learning the successful way to play a supernatural game of snakes and ladders. Rather, I conclude that finding my way as a Christian is about discovering what being 'perfect' means and how I might manage to start to be like that. Saint Augustine puts it like this: 'I do not say to thee, "Seek the way", for the Way itself has come to thee. Arise and walk!'

❧

7

My Utmost for His Highest

For the irony is, I am made only too well in thine image, the image of a jealous God (see Psalm 35).

(Wandor, 1984)

ALICE'S STORY

Her hair drooped across her shoulders, lank and listless. Her face was pale and her dull clothes looked to have come from a charity shop, seemingly chosen for their poor fit and unflattering colours rather than their suitability. On first glance at her outward appearance, I sensed that Alice might be feeling too depressed to be able to bother about looking after herself properly any longer.

My hunch was confirmed when she told me the story of the previous twenty years. She had struggled her way through university, with little money and a great deal of prayer and fasting, gained a first class degree in linguistics, then worked as a pioneer missionary overseas among people belonging to a hill tribe in an isolated part of the world. She and another single woman had been selected because they were the cream of the crop of missionary candidates in their year at the Bible college, which Alice attended straight from university. They were chosen to work together on this project, to master the language of the tribe, reduce as much of it as they could to writing and share the gospel with these people. Alice was thrilled and felt honoured to have been set apart for such a calling.

Alice's parents were eccentric but sincere Christians. She had grown up in an atmosphere in which being 'completely dedicated to God' and setting oneself apart to follow his way,

and only his, was the expected norm. Her father was idealized, seen as Godlike and above the merely human. The fact
that he spent his time (when not at his paid job) in church
relief work in the slums made him seem even more perfect
than he would otherwise have been. No one in the family
ever noticed, or admitted even to themselves, that they
wanted him to be home much more often.

'Serving God to the exclusion of all else' was modelled by
Alice's father as being the ideal way in which to live, and
'being a martyr for Christ' was the role adopted by her
mother. The arts, crafts, skills and science of 'sacrifice' were
studied and practised in that home. 'Nothing is too good for
God . . . everything must be placed on his altar as our sacrifice' was their attitude. A favourite Bible verse of theirs was 'I
appeal to you therefore brethren, by the mercies of God to
present your bodies as a living sacrifice, holy and acceptable
to God, which is your spiritual worship' (Romans 12.1). Alice
and her brothers assumed that normal Christian living was
about ensuring that nothing obstructed the 'real work' of the
one who has been privileged to have been called and separated from everyone else to serve God. 'Real' work for the
man of the house, the children learned, was nothing to do
with fathering a family; it was about serving God totally and
(in the words of the title of Alice's mother's favourite book)
giving 'my utmost for his highest'.

After three years abroad, Alice almost glimpsed that she
and her primitive, electricityless, tribal lifestyle were completely mismatched, that the loneliness of living as a for-
eigner within a close-knit tribal group near the crest of a
steep hill leached away the enthusiasm and fervour with
which she had embarked on her task, and that she and her
colleague had next to nothing in common with each other.
She really wanted a husband to satisfy her sexual longings
and to have children of her own, but the only white man to
come her way twice a year was the well-married Mission
Director, who seemed not to notice her as anything other
than a machine that translated a foreign tongue into that of
the West.

Alice shut and blinkered her inner eyes, hardened her heart, gritted her teeth and hung on silently for years as her inner despair mounted. Her mother's book title stuck in her mind and she tried to offer God 'my utmost for his highest'. As her life grew increasingly depressing and unhappy, the language she was learning and committing to paper became more understandable, so she buried herself and her real feelings in her work. She would start at dawn's first cockcrow and try to study and decipher the language without break, apart from pauses for water or tea, until dusk fell. Exhausted, she ate her bowl of rice and vegetables, then huddled in the dark on the planks of her mattressless sleeping platform until she sank into oblivion. She dare not allow herself to think or notice how she was feeling.

With the passage of months and years, her translation work progressed and a handful of tribal people became Christians. Her decision not to leave her new little flock for trips home was applauded. 'Dedicated wholly to God!' was her parents' gratified reaction to all of this. No one realized how near collapse she would be were she to leave 'the work' that had become the opiate with which she drugged the painful feelings and questions in her mind so that they had no chance to surface. It was only when the Communists overran the hills in which (what was now referred to as) 'her tribe' lived and they were driven to the plains, and she in turn was driven out of the country by the unexpected withdrawal of her work permit, that everything collapsed around her and she was forced to face issues she had never thought about before. Foremost in her mind was the question as to what it means to be 'a committed Christian and to follow God's way'. She had struggled to be and do this and now wondered whether she had been mistaken.

BEING SANCTIFIED

Teaching runs through the Old and New Testaments about God's people being set apart or sanctified. The New Testament is concerned more with the actual process of sanctifying, or of becoming sanctified, than it is with debating the

precise nature of the end product – sanctification itself. Sanctification is seen as being a process rather than a once and for
all event. In this way, sanctification is similar to being or
becoming 'perfect'. The process of being sanctified, being set
apart, becoming perfect, complete or whole, is connected
with the expectation that certain qualities will develop and
flower in our lives. Some of these qualities may seem to be
those that are apparent in God, as God is portrayed in certain
parts of the Bible. We are quick to notice when God is de-
picted as being merciful and tender and we want to 'be sanctified' and become more like the God who contains qualities
like these. We tend to ignore the uncomfortable parts of
Scripture in which God is shown to be angry, ruthless and
unjust. This perplexes us. Certain of God's qualities, as
shown in the Bible, may attract us but others may not appeal
to us any more than they do to poet Michelene Wandor. She
writes, in words Alice, the ex-missionary, might have written
(had she understood and confronted the questioning contents
of her locked heart), paradox abounding in her candour, 'I
want to be my own jealous god, you see. For the irony is, I am
made only too well in thine image, the image of a jealous God
(see Psalm 35). "The meek shall inherit the earth"? I have
not learned meekness from watching you. You say you will
hover over me, your wings giving me protection. I've got
news for you. I'm allergic to feathers!' (Wandor, 1984).

Few of us dare to be honest enough to utter words like
these. As followers of Jesus, we apparently, as part of being
sanctified, are expected to display qualities that rarely involve
'doing what comes naturally'. Qualities like meekness and
lack of jealousy are not the stuff of which most of us are really
made, despite the fact that the outer mask we tend to wear
gives an appearance to the contrary. For such qualities to be
truly *part* of ourselves, some kind of radical inner change
must occur. Exceptionally, this takes the form of a sudden
transformation (like the chronic drug-user suddenly quitting
drugs on conversion to Christ), but more commonly it is a
slow process of change that happens over a lifetime. It seems
that Jesus was not impatient about getting people to display

these desired qualities immediately, but, rather, had, and still allows, all the time in the world, and apparently anticipated that changes would develop as part of a slow, gradual process. I take heart from the saying: 'God is never in a hurry but he is never too late!'

The positive qualities to be aimed for, according to the New Testament, include such things as meekness, humility, compassion, purity, a forgiving spirit, love for enemies and so on. This is not as straightforward as might appear on casual reading of these words for Jesus was being his usual radical self. He taught his followers (among other things) about one particular quality – humility, which, he taught, was well worth emulating. However, this quality was regarded as valueless by the peoples of his time. Humility was far from being a virtue in the eyes of his Jewish and Greek contemporaries, the Greeks even going so far as to take it as a sign of weakness and, as such, treating it with contempt. Jesus also listed vices to be renounced, including among these hypocrisy, retaliation and censoriousness. All of this teaching implied that something was to take place that went beyond merely assuming an outward appearance of acting in a prescribed manner; it was to be real change springing from an inner, life-imparting well. Jesus taught that 'there is nothing outside a man, which by going into him can defile him; but the things which come out of man are what defiles him' (Mark 7.15). This suggests that it is an attitude of mind, the state of affairs in one's inner world, which is vital and from which, hopefully, will then spring the kind of actions Jesus wanted to see in his followers.

Perfection is regarded differently by different streams of Christianity. For some, 'perfection' means taking 'the evangelical counsels of perfection as binding duties' (Macquarrie and Childress, 1986), while for others it means following John Wesley's doctrine of 'perfect love', which is sometimes referred to as 'scriptural holiness'. Wesley had in mind an ideal state of affairs that he took to be a state 'of regeneration in which attitude and motive are sinless, even though conduct may be objectively faulty because of creaturely limitations and knowledge' (Macquarrie and Childress, 1986). However,

T. E. Jessop adds another helpful perspective to this in a dictionary of Christian ethics. He points out that 'in philosophical ethics the original Latin sense of *perfectio*, completeness, persists. It indicates the full development of one's distinctively human capacities, cognitive, aesthetic, moral, religious.' He reminds readers that, when taken widely, this concept was derived from Greek thought and is also used to include health and bodily perfection. Plato and Aristotle developed these ideas further in their philosophical teachings. Jessop emphasizes that these ideas later moved on from the realm of the individual to that of the collective, and points out that in 'the nineteenth century a new metaphysical turn was given to it in Hegel's doctrine of completeness as wholeness: the individual mind is an organ of the world spirit, which later presses on from potentiality to actualization and from individuality or separateness to union with the whole. Hegel held that in its moral aspect the process is achievable not in the individual but only in the social whole' (Macquarrie and Childress, 1986). Hegel's work was later developed by others who conceived perfection as self-realization and spelled this out in the Greek and Christian virtues, insisting on its social reference but preserving individuality.

Some of Jesus' demands seem near impossible for most of us, like that of voluntarily bearing a cross for the right motives: 'If any man would come after me, let him deny himself and take up his cross and follow me' (Mark 8.34). His suggestion that we should voluntarily drink the cup of suffering (Matthew 20.22) from other than masochistic motives or those of wanting to win enough extra heavenly brownie points to gain us preferential treatment by God, seems beyond most of us. Jesus searchingly asks, 'Are you able to drink the cup that I drink, or to be baptized with the baptism with which I am baptized?' (Mark 10.38). He expects the answer to be 'no!' He suggests that we are to seek a quality of living that is not that which people normally assume.

Thus, sanctification (the coming about of radical inner changes) can be seen as a process that, at times, in some individuals, could be likened to the gradual transformation that occurs when fruit and sugar are gently and slowly simmered in a pan and turn into jam. At other times, sanctification could be regarded as being like the radical metamorphosis that occurs when a butterfly bursts out of a chrysalis and is able to fly the skies or the apostle Paul emerges from the persecuting Saul under the burning, blinding light of a Damascus road. Such inner workings and transformations often require the catalytic input of disturbing rational struggles with logical thought processes at those painful moments when logic seems to defy reason. But, in many cases, if radical personality change is to occur, such thinking will be accompanied by movement, even turmoil, at an emotional level, and so it has to sink deeper than the levels of our conscious awareness, into the unconscious, unknown parts of ourselves.

WHAT HAPPENED TO ALICE

Alice realized that she was handicapped in some kind of way by her understanding of Christianity and paralysed further because she was outwardly struggling to conform to the vision she had of being as perfect as her idealized father seemed to have been. She could not live up to her aim and was unable to admit and confront this for many years. When external events forced reality to her notice, then it seemed as if her entire world fell apart and she 'broke down'. But then she began to rebuild her life until it was sounder and more profoundly Christ's in its integrity and authenticity than she had previously thought possible.

Alice's story is, I think, an exaggerated, yes, but true example of how it is for some Christians. They not only struggle to emulate the person they admire, but also assume that they can do things that would seem to be beyond the bounds of normal possibility for many other people. It is as if, because they are doing certain things 'in Christ's name', they have a right to expect to be as omnipotent as a baby or toddler feels he or she really is, until growth into adult life disillusions them and teaches them otherwise. The words of Paul, 'I can do all things through Christ who strengthens me' (Philippians

4.13), are, in my opinion, taken and used out of context at times to bolster such an assumption of infantile omnipotence in otherwise adult Christians.

THE STRUGGLE TO BE CHRISTLIKE

Different Christians struggle in different ways to try to be like the one they follow. A phenomenon that seems to me to be like a disastrous and misguided kind of spiritual one-upmanship is seen in some segments of the Church. There are certain individuals or groups of Christians who take the apostle Paul's words personally to heart and declare that, like him, they ought to be able 'to do all things through Christ who strengthens me'. So far, so good, but this is then taken further to imply that Christians, therefore, can do anything God wants them to do. Add to this a saying like the one that 'God's work, done in God's way, will never lack God's supplies' and you have a recipe for potential success or major disaster.

There are some Christians who scramble these ideas in their minds and come to think something like an assumption that, as they are following God's will (it is unquestioningly assumed that they are doing this), with Christ's Holy Spirit inside them, they will then definitely be able to carry out whatever it is that they set out to achieve. On the face of it this seems deceptively fine, but things go awry when this kind of thinking leads them also to assume that they really can do anything (go without adequate sleep, push their bodies to the limit, exhaust their family's emotional resources, deprive their loved ones of care and so on) and God will compensate for all this in some way. In some cases, it is as if they have assumed that as they have Christ within them, they themselves have somehow *become* Christ – like Christ they are omnipotent and human limitations can therefore be ignored and transcended.

When these people crash, they are surprised. No one knows, or dares to ask, who has let whom down. Is God let down by the Christians whose faith was apparently insufficient to manage to do that which they were 'called' by God to do or (usually no one dares to ask) has God let the Christians down by failing to make them immune to the limitations of being human? Their supporters may also be surprised and shocked for they may have invested much energy and resources in supporting these special Christians, whom they have idealized and whom they have set up as being set apart, idealized super-Christians. Aiming for 'perfection' as a Christian is not, in my view, about aiming to be superhuman, but, rather, aiming to find wholeness within the limitations of our humanity.

IMITATION AND IDENTIFICATION

We tend to want to be like the people who surround us or, better still, to have them be like us. As Christians, we may think that our shared faith means that we will *automatically* be like one another, in all that is important. We may assume that if we all obey Paul's injunction to 'be imitators of God, as beloved children' (Ephesians 5.1) that we will then comfortably turn out to be like each other and, therefore, free from conflict between ourselves. We may add another injunction from the apostle Paul: 'Brethren, join in imitating me, and mark those who so live as you have an example in us' (Philippians 3.17), and hope that we shall therefore be able to live in harmony and oneness. The reality, though, is that life is not like this, nor is it to be expected, for Paul himself warns us that if we follow him too closely, we will follow someone who still has his 'L' plates on – 'Not that I . . . am already perfect' (Philippians 3.12).

We want to belong and we want to feel that we are identified with one another. In Christian circles, we may call the sense of closeness that develops between us 'the unity of the Spirit' or 'the fellowship of the saints'. Identification is an important part of human development. Sigmund Freud describe it as 'the earliest expression of an emotional tie with another person' (Freud, 1921) and saw it as the primitive process by which the psyche is built up. He regarded it as an important part of development. To a Freudian, identification is a 'psychological process whereby the subject assimilates an aspect, property or attributes of another and is transformed, wholly or partially, after the model the other provides' (Laplanche and Pontialis, 1988).

To Carl Jung, identification was of more limited service. He saw it as being 'unconscious imitation'. He believed that, eventually, if we are to be ourselves, we need to shake loose the identifications of childhood. He said that 'identification can be seen as beneficial so long as the individual cannot go his own way. But when a better possibility presents itself, identification shows its morbid character by becoming just as great a hindrance as it was an unconscious help and support before' (Jung, 1978). To some modern Jungians, identification is 'a process by which a person fuses or confuses his own identity with someone else's' (Gordon, 1978). Jung also described identification as a process that could be applied to parts of oneself (rather than to the whole of a person or thing). This means that it is possible for someone to identify with one attribute of theirs and think that this is what they are really like. This produces a lopsided view of oneself. The way in which some Christian subcultures produce people who, often in God's name, wear similar clothes, live in similar houses, have similar ethical and moral values and speak similar jargonese may be attributed as much to the unconscious effects of the processes of identification as to the work of the Holy Spirit in God's people. And who is to say that the Holy Spirit cannot work through unconscious processes as effectively as through conscious ones?

Neville Symington, who knows nothing of the real Alice and of her identification with her father, writes in psychoanalytical language of the kind of thing that I think happened to her. I think that his words apply to a process that is also familiar to some who study some church cultures. He explains that such idealization of someone (in this case I am thinking of Alice's father) 'is always accompanied by a process of primary identification'. Those doing the idealizing will identify with the object by submerging themselves in it and assuming 'the cloak, outlook, vision, hearing, smell, taste, and touch of the idealized object, which is always defended with a paranoid passion ... with idealization there is always identification and an omnipotence, which replaces the subject's individual learning and experience. Paradoxically, humility is the bedfellow of personal experience, and omnipotence companion to knowledge that has come about through identification with a hero' (Symington, 1986). He points out that Fairbairn, an important Scottish psychoanalyst, believed that the earliest relationship of infancy sprung from just such an identification. When things work out well, this unequal relationship develops into a mature relationship of dependency between two independent individuals who are able to develop and become themselves and to be their own people. However, things do not always work out in this way. If 'traumatic disappointment takes place then the person stays emotionally stuck at the stage of primary identification. This state of affairs is the same as what today is more commonly called the narcissistic state' (Symington, 1986). Churches have more than their fair share of people who are narcissistically wounded and who are, therefore, susceptible to being particularly hurt when ideals are not met and when omnipotence does not work out.

Symington suggests that healing can sometimes occur within some such people in the context of certain relationships. I see this occurring at times within the relationship offered by a counsellor or a therapist, who finds that he or she is acting *in loco parentis* as far as the inner world of the person who comes to them is concerned. On occasion, a similar relationship may spring up within a church context in which a senior church member may become like a father or mother to someone. This is harder to manage, unless the pastoral carer has some training to enable them to understand what may be going on and stick with it. However, it is sometimes through such a relationship, that of being like the 'primary love object' (a baby's main care-giver), that it sometimes seems that the Holy Spirit is able to move and to bring healing to the damaged and 'split' internal world of some adults. Symington points out that the damage originally done in infancy 'begins to be repaired as a patient can feel safe enough to make emotional contact again with a figure in the real world. . . . Emotional contact with a real person is the medicine which heals the deep splits in the personality. The resistance to this healing process . . . is the patient's violent resistance to emotional closeness. It is the absence of closeness which has been the cause of such pain and suffering as at a forgotten period of childhood' (Symington, 1986).

Alice followed her family pattern of seeking to be 'set apart for God' to give 'my utmost for his highest', but she was forced, in mid-life, to examine what she had got right and what she had got wrong in the way she had tried to do this. One of the problems she had to grapple with was that of trying to understand how much sanctification is something that we can achieve by our own efforts and how much it is something that is brought about in us. In other words, are we 'sanctified by works or by grace?'

8

True Glory

People made in the image of God are to shine with reflected but real light.

(Oppenheimer, in, Macquarrie and Childress, 1986)

SAM'S STORY

Sam would never have thought of himself as being like the fairy-tale character Little Red Riding Hood, but that's how I see him these days, even though he is male and in his mid-fifties. There is something both endearing and frightening about Sam's apparent naivety and trustful nature. It is frightening if, as a colleague or relative of his, you need to rely on him to watch out for your welfare.

All his adult life, Sam has donned his metaphorical red cloak – red, the colour of roses that say 'I love you!' – and ventured out into woods and forests all over the world. He was once nearly lost in a deserted South American plain when his horse bolted off into shrubland far from the main party. Another time, oblivious of any peril, he missed the dangerous bullets in an African war zone when the travel permits of all foreigners were withdrawn on safety grounds. A police road block saved him from being taken hostage by a guerrilla band in another African country. He avoided being caught in the ravages of mountain flooding in Nepal because his long-planned trip to that land began just ten days after devastating monsoon rains. And so the story of Red Riding Hood's travels continue, with him being oblivious of peril and there being apparently one near-miss after another, living happily ever after.

Strangely, to some pairs of eyes other than his, he seems not to have noticed the dangers through which he has passed.

His motto is: 'God has sent me and so God will keep me safe!' His scarlet, loving cloak (red, the colour of courage as well as of love) cocoons him from life's nasties. Its high collar (when pulled up high enough) acts as a blinker so that he does not see anything other than that which he has gone to see. Should the pressure mount above his comfort level, Sam curls up on the ground, his cloak now serving as bedding, mentally anaesthetizes himself and sleeps his way through the stressful situation. By the time he wakes up someone else has organized calm again.

This Red Riding Hood has spent many years of his life taking his basket full of medicines, food and clothes to the poor and starving of the world. He knows the needy grannies in all their guises, from orphaned refugee babies to deformed, leprous youths or AIDS sufferers. He tirelessly visits remote Third World hospitals and clinics, he encourages relief workers and infuses some of his red blood into their exhausted veins by his faith and optimism, and he walks knee-deep through the mud and stench of the most wretched of refugee and displaced persons camps. His twice-yearly travels to, and through, the woods of the world, bearing his basket of provisions for each year's needy granny, make worth while the daily routine, the humdrum work of buying, pricing, preparing the supplies, raising funds and sitting on the endless boring councils and committees that are the price he pays for the work he loves. He is unaware that, as Elizabeth Bowen comments, 'sacrificers are not the ones to pity. The ones to pity are those they sacrifice' (Bowen, 1990).

In the perseverance of this daily grind, broken only by his excitement when another traveller calls to visit him and to share his sandwich lunch, Sam's character has been shaped. There is a process at work in him in which different aspects of his personality are being changed, healed and unified. I might call this in religious language 'sanctification' or in psychological language 'integration' or 'increasing self-awareness and self-acceptance'.

Sam is, however, barely aware of the flip side of his open, loving, trustful nature. He does not really notice that, on more than two occasions, when he has ventured forth on a major new project (with a joyful desire to give himself totally to God, to hold nothing back, in serving God through serving others), the end result has been that he has landed up in bed with a sharp-toothed wolf rather than the granny who was to have protected and nurtured him in return for his consecration to God. His friends, aware of his tendency to repeat this pattern, bale him out and set his feet on a new path, hoping each time that he will not, yet again, fail to investigate before embarking on his journey whether or not a granny can be guaranteed to be at his destination rather than a wolf who will hurt and then discard him. Sam found it nearly impossible to grasp the fact that, in some instances, these 'wolves' were Christians, to whom he had trusted himself and his welfare, people who had assured him that they prayed regularly for him. And yet, despite and through it all, a process I call 'sanctification' is proceeding inside him.

Sam, since his student days, saw himself as called, consecrated and set apart to the service of God. He determined that God's commands and demands on his life should take priority over all other commitments. 'God first, others second, self last!' was one of the mottoes by which he tried to live. On the face of it, this seemed laudable to those among his friends who believed that looking after oneself is the last thing to be done. His wife and children sometimes felt guilty when they noticed how much they resented that their needs for Sam's attention went unmet, for God always got in first and was given the lion's share of what Sam had to offer.

There were times when his friends wished *they* could dedicate themselves to God as wholeheartedly as Sam did. There were, however, other moments that confused them. These were those occasions when they secretly wondered whether all was exactly as it appeared to be. Their unspoken questions centred on their sense that it might be possible that, sometimes, when Sam confidently asserted 'God has told me to do this and so I must obey!', he might be wrong. They felt guilty for doubting him and for wondering whether or not (without realizing what he was doing) Sam might have *assumed* that God had told him to do something when, in fact, God was not too bothered about the matter but, rather, it was something that *Sam* was determined to do. This was a simple, question-proof method of getting his own way and of getting his friends to support him in doing whatever it was. His friends could not argue with his conviction for, when they were honest with themselves, they knew that they did not hear God's voice as certainly or as clearly as Sam appeared to. They felt inferior in the face of his apparent prayer hotline to God. As he seemed to be a Christian of superior standing to them, who were they to argue with him? His unchurched friends were puzzled by all of this, and in their exasperation used words and phrases among themselves to describe him like 'arrogant', 'know-it-all' and 'powerful manipulator'.

MORE THOUGHTS ON SANCTIFICATION

The Christian idea of 'sanctification' is an important one for Sam. The roots of the concept of sanctification sink far back into human history and lie deep in the concept of setting someone or something apart, usually for the sole use of the Judaeo-Christian God or the god or goddess of another religion or for the purposes of religious ritual.

The Greek word used in the New Testament, *hagiozo*, is commonly used to mean to 'consecrate', 'make sacred' and 'sanctify'. Jesus uses the Greek word derived from *hagiozo* in a couple of different ways. He uses it to refer to a technicality when he asks, making his point in an argument, 'which is greater, the gold or the temple that has made the gold sacred?' (Matthew 23.16). He also uses it when he speaks about his supreme consecration of himself. In his words relating to his followers, in his great prayer before his crucifixion, he asks that God will 'sanctify them in the truth; thy word is truth. As you didst send me into the world, so I have sent them into the world. And for their sake I consecrate myself, that they also may be consecrated in truth' (John 17.7–15).

I am struck here by the emphasis Jesus places on truth, on integrity. He requests that his followers shall be 'consecrated in truth'. I believe that it is our responsibility to grasp the truth as clearly as we are able. On many occasions, our perception of truth is distorted by unseen, unconscious factors. We *think* we understand and know, yet we cannot know those things of which we are as yet unaware, the things that are not known to our rational thinking selves. To me, the vital ingredient in our becoming 'truthful' is our determined attempt to make conscious as much unconscious material as we are able to. One of my friends once suggested that an important aspect of 'sinning' might be our failure to try to discover and work with some of the hidden aspects of our inner selves. As we do this, so our inner and outer realities and truths will the more nearly match and approximate each other.

'You, therefore, must be perfect, as your heavenly Father is perfect!' declares Jesus (Matthew 5.48). As we ponder further, we are likely to be confronted by the question 'When Jesus commands us to be 'perfect' (a concept like 'set apart' and 'to be holy'), is this something we should *be*, instantly, or *become* or do his words contain a promise that this is a state to be attained at some future time (after we have died)?' We also face questions about whether or not Jesus is employing the linguistic device he sometimes used of overstating his point, using hyperbole to make sure that his hearers get the point. In this case, he might then be saying that they are, at the very least, to be 'better than average'. This latter point of view carries an assumption that a state of being *less* than perfect is acceptable. Further, we may find ourselves puzzling, as others have down the centuries, as to whether or not this desirable state of 'perfection' or 'sanctification' is something we can achieve by our own efforts or is bestowed on us as a gift from God. How good do we have to be to be good enough for God?

The Sam version of Little Red Riding Hood shows me a man who is confused. He is struggling to be 'better than average', to be 'consecrated to God' and, in his own way, be 'perfect'. He is helping out as many grannies as he possibly can and, incidentally, gets some immediate reward for his

efforts in the form of people thinking of him as a nice person
and feeling the warm glow he always feels when he is kind
and beneficent to others. However, life conspires against his
efforts and all this by throwing him into the jaws of wolves
who tear him to shreds, chew the remains and force him to
extend his claws in return. This then wars with his view of
himself as 'nice, kind Red Riding Hood', for nice people (he
believes) do not scratch or have aggressive and destructive
feelings – especially when they are trying to be extra loving to
those in great need! He tries to neutralize his resentment and
anger by clutching at any straws he finds in Jesus' words, and
turns 'treating others as you would have them treat you' into
'be as nice to others as you would have them be nice to you!'
But, even then, if he were able to be conscious of what is
going on, he would discover that it does not quite work out as
he thought it should. In response to his kindness and gener-
osity, he is taken advantage of over and over again and left
with uncomfortable, disconcerting feelings that he had no
idea could possess him – feelings that are the opposite of
those he has as he sets out on his mercy mission. True to
form, he disposes of such feelings as best he can; they are not
examined in the light of day nor seen for what they are. His
approach is to do his best to find peace and quiet, and he does
this by ignoring any upsetting implications of what is happening to him.

I find different versions of Sam sitting in many of the pews
in our churches – kind, well-meaning people who are taken
advantage of, get hurt in the process and make out that it does
not really matter. However, at times, I also see an inner process at work in many, so that unwanted and unacceptable
feelings of resentment and bitterness are owned and recognized for what they are; they are brought to the surface of
conscious awareness, struggled with and, then, a quality akin
to agape love sometimes breaks forth, like a snowdrop
through icy winter snow. I call this a kind of metamorphosis,
and I also call this 'sanctification'. However, this is less simple
than I make it sound.

SOME OTHER APPROACHES

Theologian Helen Oppenheimer tackles the subject in a way that I find helpful. She expresses her opinion in the paradox that 'sanctification cannot be considered optional; but to treat it as compulsory can be just as misleading' (Macquarrie and Childress, 1986). To my mind, such a paradox cannot be tidied away in a neat package of beliefs. It must be viewed from all angles, with the understanding that the view at eye level may appear so totally different to that of an aerial view that the picture then comes to be seen as something quite different. Thus, what seems logically impossible may, contrary to reason, make perfect sense to another part of myself.

Oppenheimer points out that attempts to make sense of the paradox that sanctification is neither optional nor compulsory have led to the development of many different possible ways of trying to find a solution. This has resulted in there being 'plenty of available heresies, Catholic and Protestant, mostly brandishing proof texts' (Macquarrie and Childress, 1986). She points out, for instance, that, on the one hand, the presence of a belief in the doctrine of 'compulsory sanctification develops the rigorism that requires Christians to be sinless on pain of rejection' (Macquarrie and Childress, 1986) while, on the other, there is 'the superstition that supposes that grace works like magic' (Macquarrie and Childress, 1986). Between the two is 'optional sanctification', which 'allows the anti-nomianism that justifies sinners and stops there, or the worldliness that asks only for decent behaviour and hardly cares for holiness' (Macquarrie and Childress, 1986). An acquaintance of Sam's stated, perplexed, 'He says he's saved by grace, but I've never seen anyone work so hard to earn his salvation, to earn his wholeness'.

These are some of the reasons for Helen Oppenheimer stating that some people have resorted to finding other ways of working through the maze these matters create. Thus, one particular group of Christians attack concepts about perfectionism 'as arrogant, its denial as defeatist' (Macquarrie and Childress, 1986). Another way, adopted by others, is that of postulating the validity of their particular hypothesis, which could be seen to be either a 'safety net, or a snare, of a doctrine of two standards, a minimum for all and a better way for some' (Macquarrie and Childress, 1986). Thus, celibacy is regarded as a 'better way for some' in certain segments of the Church and faithfulness within marriage is the 'minimum' requirement 'for all'. She suggests that this may be 'an understandable expedient to avoid legalistic rigorism, but desperately unsatisfactory as a self-sufficient theory' (Macquarrie and Childress, 1986). I agree with her belief that 'it is essential to hold on to the understanding that sanctity is for everyone and that somehow, explain it as we may, morals constitute a preamble to beatitude' (Macquarrie and Childress, 1986).

Evangelicalism over the years has struggled with questions about sanctification and holiness. On a world-wide scale, in countries as far apart as Rwanda, the United States of America, China, Latin America, Korea and Scotland, to mention but a few, so-called 'holiness movements' emerged as a result. When I was a medical student in London, we Christian Union members were confused as to whether or not the so-called 'Keswick Convention' teaching (with its emphasis on the idea that the essential precursor to holiness was complete surrender of oneself to God) was the *only* way in which we could be sanctified. Life became, for some Christians, a frustrating, failure-dogged attempt to 'give everything to God'. Sinful actions were sure signs that one's consecration was somehow deficient. Life became a grind of trying to be completely given over to God and of swimming against the current that bore one helplessly, almost remorselessly, in the direction of committing yet another sinful deed, which in turn marked yet another failure to master this complete dedication, which, some believed, was the guarantee of sinless living. Some kind of 'second blessing' experience, a very special experience of rededication of oneself to God, which was almost akin to a second conversion, for some people held out the hope of receiving an inner, powerful, Holy Spirit-driven supermotor that would enable them to swim effortlessly upstream against the fiercest torrents, never sinning again.

Historian Balleine, writing about the movement in the United States from which the Keswick Convention developed, said 'Their method was mysticism run mad . . . they urged their converts to stand up and "profess Sanctification", then and there to yield their bodies to the Holy Ghost, and to believe that from that moment they could never sin again' (Parsons, 1988). To many church people, such teaching about 'sinless perfection was deemed to be a dangerous doctrine from which godly people needed protection' (Parsons, 1988). The first annual Keswick Convention was held in 1875, and it grew to attract an attendance of about 10,000 people each summer. The evangelical leaders tried to monitor the proceedings responsibly 'lest the supercharged atmosphere in which it operated encouraged error as well as excess' (Parsons, 1988). The paper in which the proceedings were published, *The Record*, 'fearing the substitution of personal holiness for Christ's atoning sacrifice, warned against the confusion of sanctification with justification. The latter, its readers were reminded, was imputed, not imparted; the former, a cumulative development, was attained by the leading of the Holy Spirit within the soul' (Parsons, 1988). For many Christians, attending Keswick Convention meetings (in my student days, the after-meetings with their emphasis on the need to specially receive God's power in order to be holy through total dedication of oneself to God) was similar to their initial challenge to follow Christ completely and was experienced as a second conversion experience, although the organizers did not express it in such terms.

As a student, approaches to 'holy living' other than that taught at Keswick were also being preached. In my heart, a flame had been kindled, a vision glimpsed, a hope yearned for, which was that the piety of those who walked in the 'Keswick' way could be mine. I admired some of the godly, wise older men and women who had followed this path. Their gentle characters, simple faith and shining faces attracted me. It does not surprise me, therefore, looking back, to realize that this was one of the factors that led me as an idealistic teenager to dedicate my life to missionary service and choose to offer myself to God through one of those 'faith' missionary societies whose leadership and inspiration had sprung from the well of the Keswick Convention teachings. My later disappointment came when I was forced to realize that this particular way of being did not work for me as I had hoped it would. I was disillusioned by my manifest inability to be as holy as I had set out to be, and was inwardly furious both with myself and with others for what seemed to be the way in which I had been misled.

SOME ANSWERS?

The fact that 'holiness movements' offer different recipes for Christians to attain holiness suggests to me that no one movement has found the answer. Time and time again, down the ages and across the world, sincere Christians struggle with these issues, trying out one approach and then another, but no solution has been found that guarantees Christians a completely holy way of living. This suggests to me that we need to find another way of understanding the biblical teaching enjoining Christians to be holy.

Challenging words in the Bible seem to apply to all believers – words like 'I am the Lord your God; consecrate yourselves therefore, and be holy, for I am holy' (Leviticus 11.44). 'As he who called you is holy, be holy yourselves in all your conduct; since it is written, "You shall be holy, for I am holy"' (1 Peter 1.16). The Bible gives no indication that such commands apply exclusively to first-class, aristocratic Christians while second-class, run-of-the-mill, ordinary folk are exempt. Helen Oppenheimer asserts that 'what matters is that we set no limits upon the ultimate capacity of God's creatures to glorify God: to take seriously the idea that "you are holy, for I am holy" is meant to be fulfilled. To stop short with justified sinners is no more adequate than to celebrate an aristocracy of blessedness' (Macquarrie and Childress, 1986).

Some of the Old Testament characters are described as being 'blameless', in terms reminiscent of the New Testament teaching about being 'perfect'. Noah 'was a righteous man, blameless in his generation; Noah walked with God' (Genesis 6.5). Job, too, was portrayed by God as being 'a blameless and upright man, who fears God and turns away from evil' (Job 1.1). Abraham was urged by God to 'walk before me, and be blameless' (Genesis 17.1). The Israelites were commanded 'you shall be blameless before the Lord your God' (Deuteronomy 18.13).

The Hebrew word *tam* or *tamin* is translated as 'blameless', but has lying behind it another word, which means 'basically complete, possessing integrity'. However, theologian Francis Wright Beare suggests that 'the words should not be interpreted as demanding our best human effort to attain the unattainable, but rather our "total engagement" without half-measures or reserves' (Wright Beare, 1981). Here is another of God's paradoxes, yet another example of God holding opposites in tension, where both 'this' is true and, at the same time, its opposite, 'that', is equally valid. And so, in the letter to the Philippians, Christians are told to 'work out your own salvation with fear and trembling; for God is at work in you, both to will and to work for his good pleasure' (Philippians 2.12, 13).

I see in the quest of many people undergoing psychoanalysis a searching for the holy grail of wholeness, completion and healing that seems to me to be very similar to the process referred to in the Bible as 'sanctification'. Church of England clergyman Christopher Bryant found that 'one of the truths that Jung has brought home to me is that the search for individuation, for wholeness, is in no way incompatible with but is rather complementary to the quest for union with God' (Bryant, 1983). This idea is not as new as it may sound. Several hundreds of years ago, the sage Irenaeus expressed his understanding that 'the glory of God is man fully alive'. To psychotherapists and many counsellors, the insights of psychology offer the potential to free people from the grip of that which is unconscious and allow them to discover the freedom to live fully.

Red Riding Hood needs his cloak and basket for they serve as the outer marks of his identity. Yet, underneath and inside this unusual man lies not only a gentle heart, but the aggression of which few (even the wolves) are aware. Even fewer people guess that the cloak was assumed out of necessity in infancy to protect and hide an inner little baby – red from screaming in terror, rage and despair at the way in which he was mishandled. This was the way in which he learned from experience how to cope with life from infancy onwards.

All of us have our own inner babies and children who, from time to time, require our attention. One of the most wonderful things that can happen to people is for them to find and become their true selves. Then, gently and in safety, at times, they can come out from behind the protective cloak of their false self and discover their hidden, vulnerable and precious true self. The protective cloak enables us to cope but, like a cape, covers something that is rarely seen. It seems to me that to become 'fully alive', as Iranaeus suggests people can become, is to discover one's inner self and openly allow it to be part of oneself (with its inevitable shamefully embarrassing warts and all) and this can then be 'the glory of God'.

This can be seen to be part of the process of sanctification. T. W. Manson puts it this way: 'To follow Christ is not to go in pursuit of an ideal but to share in the results of an achievement' (Guthrie, 1981). While Augustine made a similar point in one of his favourite comments on Jesus' question, '"What have you that you did not receive?" and summed the matter up in the words: "When God crowns our merits, he crowns nothing but his own gifts"' (Macquarrie and Childress, 1986). Thus, sanctification can be seen in terms of being like the reaping of a harvest, the flowering and then the fruiting that is of the Holy Spirit. 'The fruit of the Spirit is love, joy, peace, patience, kindness, goodness, faithfulness, gentleness, self-control' (Galatians 5.22, 23). As Helen Oppenheimer puts it, 'People made in the image of God are to shine with reflected but real light' (Macquarrie and Childress, 1986).

I believe that what we are to aspire to is something that is always on the move. It is thus indefinable and elusive, constantly changing form, shape and colour and ebbing and flowing like a tidal river. It is not readily contained and set solid in the concrete of one clear concept or fixed, unmoving, unrippled like the surface of a stagnant pond. It may well be that sanctification follows a path like that of Hegel's dialectic. This suggests that when *one thing* is combined with *another* then *something else* results, but this *something else* does not stay exactly as it was when it was first formed for it soon becomes another *one thing*. This, before long, is added to *another* to produce a fresh *something else*! In the ancient wisdom of Gregory of Nyassa, 'The perfection of human nature consists perhaps in its very growth in goodness . . . the continual development of life to what is better is the soul's way to perfection' (Macquarrie and Childress, 1986).

Those of us who have embarked on a journey of inner understanding and change may find strength and encouragement if we are able to sense that this is part of God's calling to us. Those involved in an internal journey and process of change through psychotherapy may be able to see that the Holy Spirit works through unconscious processes and uses the training and insights of a therapist in the same way that the early physicians claimed that they might administer 'the medicine but it is God that brings the healing'. Carl Jung understood the human psyche to be working towards finding integration and saw this movement towards wholeness as being a natural growth process. But it is a journey of which we are naturally fearful for it involves our facing and coming to terms with aspects of ourselves that we have automatically banished from consciousness, for they embarrass, disgust or terrify us. I believe this to be part of our moving towards wholeness, holiness, integration and sanctification.

I admire and am exasperated by the man Red Riding Hood. He has the marks of a saint, a set apart one, but he also sometimes seems so innocent and naive that I lose patience with him. Perhaps he is one of those holy ones of whom Karl Barth says 'holy in the Bible does not mean devout or virtuous but separated by God' (Macquarrie and Childress, 1986).

Taking up the ideas of separation and sacrifice, Helen Oppenheimer makes a suggestion worthy of time and thought. She says that 'the consecration of a sacrificial offering can mean more than the propitiation of incomprehensible powers. When the human impulse to consecrate a sacrifice is allowed to develop in the context of *sacrament* and indeed of *eucharist*, the ethical meaning of "sanctification" can be removed from the optional/compulsory trap and associated with grace, gift, and thanksgiving. To be sanctified is to be offered like the elements of a sacrament, to be blessed and given back to nourish other people' (Macquarrie and Childress, 1986).

Perhaps the man Red Riding Hood understands better than me that 'the glory of God is man fully alive'. He has separated himself, consecrated himself and offered himself 'to be blessed and given back to nourish other people'. That he is human and his offering is intertwined with human bungles, messes and confusions does not completely invalidate what he does. There is further mystery in the way in which God uses people regardless of whether or not their motives are completely 'pure' – and how can we possibly be human and not act out of mixed motives most of the time?

9

Sin and Symbols

The spiritual guides of the Eastern Orthodox Churches describe true prayer as holding the mind in the heart.

(Bryant, 1983)

SANDRA'S STORY

There was something about herself that had bothered Sandra for many years. She was married, comfortably well off and held down a secure hospital job, which she enjoyed most of the time. She found it almost impossible to get to the bottom of what it was that kept on undermining her intentions to be a certain kind of person. She *intended* to be woman of integrity and did not want to be dishonest, but she tended to pick up and collect odd things that really belonged to other people. She preferred not to notice, let alone think about this too deeply.

As a little girl, Sandra had, from time to time, secretly rummaged through her mother's handbag and sneaked out small items, like a lipstick or a comb, and low denomination coins that would not be missed. Now, as an adult, sometimes she found herself concealing and taking home the occasional box of tissues from the rest room of the restaurant where she was having lunch or going home hiding a roll of toilet paper from the hospital where she worked in her shopping basket or secreting in her bag a valueless ballpoint pen from the bank where she had an account. She could not understand her tendency to pinch small items. 'After all,' she would chide herself, 'It's not as if you can't afford to buy these things for yourself – you can!'

For years, Sandra managed to escape paying attention to what she was doing. On the rare occasions when she thought

about it, she hated and despised herself for being so silly.
How could any adult like herself be unable to control a desire
to steal something so small and worthless? If she had stolen
vast sums of money or jewellery, she would have been more
understanding of herself. As it was, she felt too perplexed to
explore the possible meanings of what she was doing. She
noticed that there were moments when she would be overcome by an inner urge or a fleeting impulse to walk off with
something of little financial value. Time and time again, she
found that she gave in to the impulse, acting blindly and
without giving the matter thought. She hated herself for
being like this and was anxious in case anyone should discover what she was like and see this side of herself. How
could she ever admit to anyone that she, a respected, competent, professional woman, was at times overcome by an
impulse to steal a roll of toilet paper? 'It's all so childish!' she
rebuked herself.

Time and time again, she asked God to forgive her and
give her enough strength to stop stealing small things she did
not really need, but, time and time again, the cycle was repeated. She hated herself for being unable to obey what
seemed to be a straightforward commandment in the Bible,
'Thou shalt not steal'. 'Surely,' she mused, 'I ought to be able
to obey this commandment and manage not to steal paper-
clips.' But, in the event, she could not curb her impulses. She
was frustrated and furious with herself about the situation.

In mid-life, Sandra started having psychotherapy and,
through painstaking and painful work, began to understand
some of the unconscious reasons that might be driving her to
steal inconsequential items and why it was likely that this
situation had arisen in the first place. Her growing self-
awareness and understanding made her more compassionate
towards herself, less critical, and she was able to find more
appropriate and satisfying ways of meeting those needs that,
unconsciously, she had attempted to meet by stealing.

As she began to explore herself through therapy, Sandra
came to see that these needs had started off in infancy. She
had needed far more time and attention than her busy doctor

mother could give to her, the eldest of four children. The second child, an adorable and much-loved little boy, was born when Sandra was only fourteen months old. As a child, stealing from her mother's handbag had been an unconscious attempt to compensate for her need for far more of her mother. As an adult, a similar pattern had developed when she was deprived in some way, although she was not aware that this was so. She began to realize that some of the occasions when she pilfered coincided with times when she had failed to notice that she was feeling dissatisfied with work or that the person with whom she was having a meal in a restaurant was not giving her the undivided attention she had expected and that she craved. This understanding of herself, and her growing ability to recognize her need to be noticed, understood and nurtured, led her to find other ways in which her needs could be met and, some time later, she noticed with surprise that she had stopped petty thieving completely.

Sandra was fortunate to be in a position where she was able to undertake an inner spiritual or psychological journey of self-discovery with someone who was professionally trained to help her along her way. One of the benefits of her discoveries was that she found she was no longer powerlessly held in the grip of the unconscious compulsion that drove her to steal small items. Understanding the origin of the compulsion, how it had been perpetuated out of unacknowledged childhood needs for more of her mother than she had been able to get, noticing the painful and disturbing feelings associated with this and allowing this awareness to be examined consciously, proved transforming for Sandra. This may make the way in which she received the healing she required sound very simple, a kind of fairy story: with the waving of a magic wand and a 'Hey presto', she lived happily ever after. However, this is far from the truth. Yes, she was freed from her compulsion to thieve, but with the growing understanding she was beginning to gain of herself, other avenues of her inner self were opened up, demanding exploration. Hers was no instant solution to all her inner problems.

QUICK FIXES?

Some forms of 'Christian' counselling appear to offer the kind of instant relief from inner conflict for which we comfort-seeking humans naturally yearn and some people do find what they are seeking. Sadly, for others, the relief may be brief and then fade, leaving them wondering what is the matter with them and why they are not good enough to have warranted a permanent fixing of their problems by God via their sessions of 'healing ministry'. They may gaze longingly in the direction of those fortunate others who seem to be the recipients of some kind of spiritual 'zapping', whose problems apparently disappear as a result of magic-working prayer, with or without the 'laying on of hands', being 'slain in the Spirit' or an episode of 'speaking in tongues'. Some long to be like these fortunate others and are bitterly disappointed that these others have something they seem unable to receive.

Clearly, from time to time, radical inner change does occur, due to the upward, outward, expressive rush to the surface of bottled-up emotions, and this sometimes follows sessions of special prayer for healing. Like a cork is reshaped by striking the ceiling after exploding out of a shaken bottle of champagne, so an outburst of repressed, denied, hidden, previously unacknowledged emotion can shake the inner status quo in such a disturbing way that nothing is ever quite the same inside ever again; a new kind of wholeness takes shape.

The psychological process called 'catharsis' or 'abreaction' appears to be one of the ways in which immediate healing comes to a limited number of people through certain large, church-related healing meetings, small services or one-to-one pastoral encounters. The Greek word *catharsis* means 'purification' or 'purging'. Aristotle noticed that *catharsis* sometimes happened to the spectators of stage dramas – the profound tragedy they were watching stirring correspondingly deep feelings of pity and fear in members of the audience, who would then predictably release these emotions while watching the play.

In the early days of their work, pioneer psychoanalysts like Sigmund Freud used hypnosis to enable patients to connect with buried emotions and memories of long-forgotten events that had led to problems in later life. In his early work, Freud tried to enable his patients to remember – even, at times, relive – the traumatic event or events that were the precipitating cause of the present problems. His work was like that of a detective. He patiently and carefully worked with his patients to notice and follow even the smallest of clues that might be given through dreams, slips of the tongue and so on, to see whether these would lead them to understand what might have happened and connect with the hidden emotions that had proved so disturbing that they had had to be obliterated. This often led to freedom from symptoms (Laplanche and Pontialis, 1988).

A MORE LONG-TERM SOLUTION

All this was uphill work and, as psychoanalyst Bruno Bettelheim explains, it is not an easy undertaking 'to become acquainted with the lowest depths of the soul – to explore whatever personal hell we may suffer from' (Bettelheim, 1991). In his writings about Sigmund Freud, who fearlessly undertook a personal and arduous struggle to achieve greater and greater self-awareness, Bettelheim explains that this kind of inner work may seem a frightening enterprise, but he is sure that 'Freud's findings . . . give us the confidence that this demanding and potentially dangerous voyage of self-discovery will result in our becoming more fully human' (Bettelheim, 1991). He sees our being 'more fully human' in terms of our 'no longer being enslaved without knowing it to the dark forces that reside in us' (Bettelheim, 1991) and suggests that 'by exploring and understanding the origins and the potency of these forces, we not only become much better able to cope with them but also gain a much deeper and more compassionate understanding of our fellow man' (Bettelheim, 1991).

So, the guiding principle behind psychotherapy is that, in order for us to know ourselves, we need to know as much of our unconscious as we are able to at any one moment in time. If we understand some of the processes that are going on

inside and are familiar and at home with some of the unconscious factors that drive us in certain directions, then we
are less likely to be driven by these hidden factors to do or say
things that are detrimental to ourselves or other people. An
amazing change often occurs when some of the unconscious
factors that have governed our behaviour, over which we
seem to have no control, see the light of consciousness. We
may have felt defeated and out of control when we are driven
to do certain things that we have consciously decided to
avoid. However, when some of the unconscious drives are
perceived for what they are, and thus are brought in touch
with our rational minds and our thought processes, we are
then likely to find that we are able to choose whether or not to
act in certain ways; we are no longer driven to act in ways we
deplore. In Bettelheim's words, 'When we are able to confront dark forces with the powers of our rational mind,
unencumbered by unconscious pressures, then rationality
wins out; and when rationality dominates our actions, we can
overcome the destructive powers and free ourselves of their
ability to harm us' (Bettelheim, 1991).

I think that the apostle Paul was struggling with problems
similar to those faced by Sandra, Sigmund Freud and count-
less Christians and non-Christians throughout the ages.
Indeed, these are problems common to all of us for they are
part of being human. In his letter to the Romans, Paul refers
to the problem of our inability at times to live up to what we
have determined to be, in terms of our being deflected from
our course by 'sin'. A psychologist seeking to express something similar might use words like 'the shadow' or 'unconscious drives'. Paul expresses how he is perplexed about this
matter and writes fully about it. He asks, 'How can we who
died to sin still live in it?' (Romans 6.2) and 'We know that
our old self was crucified with him so that the sinful body
might be destroyed, and we might no longer be enslaved to
sin. For he who died is freed from sin' (Romans 6.6–7), as well
as 'So you also must consider yourselves dead to sin' (Romans
6.11), 'For sin will no longer have dominion over you'
(Romans 6.14) and 'But now you have been set free from sin'

(Romans 6.22). He therefore urges, 'Let not sin therefore reign in your mortal bodies, to make you obey their passions' (Romans 6.12).

As I read Paul's letter, I am able to translate his words into the kind of language Sandra used when she told me about the way in which she discovered how she did not have to remain forever enslaved to her impulse to thieve. Paul asserts that we are not doomed to spend our entire lives enslaved by sin – it is possible for us to be freed from the compulsive grip sin has on us. In religious language this may be expressed as being able 'to triumph over sin'. In the words of the old 'CSSM' chorus, some Christians sing confidently that they are 'on the victory side'. Paul makes a confident assertion of what he expects of Christians in the ability that is apparently theirs to be free of sin's domination and drives. But it is less than clear whether or not Paul is also claiming that it is within the realm of possibility for Christians to attain such a state of perfection that sin is effectively completely banished from their inner selves. Evangelical theologian Donald Guthrie, commenting on these words, suggests that 'it is unnecessary to suppose that the answer must be in the affirmative, for the key to the understanding of these statements is that sin is no longer master. It has met its match. Man is no longer a vassal to sin, but has become a slave to God. Yet he still needs urging to avoid obedience to sin' (Guthrie, 1981).

It is the experience of some Christians who have been in psychotherapy for themselves that, on many occasions, the work they do in therapy resembles that done by an honest, open, heart-searching Bible study group or that done in a deep spiritual discussion with an intimate spiritual leader or a spiritual director. The initial and hardest work, which may take a very long time, involves removing the mind's blinkers, being able to do away with some of the defensive strategies we use unconsciously and which keep us from facing certain unpalatable truths, being able to acknowledge and face up to some of the uncomfortable, unwanted, despised aspects of ourselves which we tend to conceal from others and evade exploring for ourselves.

Some Christian thinkers have tried to bring together insights gained from their understanding of spirituality and psychology. The clergyman Christopher Bryant, among others, notes similarities between Jungian thought and some aspects of the Christian way. The Jungian concept that the process of individuation is part of the psyche's natural development can be seen as having some parallels with the Christian's spiritual search for oneness with God. Bryant points out that for Carl Jung, one of the necessary first stages towards growing into increasing self-awareness is 'confrontation with the shadow, the elements in an individual which he feels to be bad and to be rejected. This teaching resembles that of the old guides who insisted that the spiritual novice must face and battle manfully with the image of sin within him, for this conflict is an essential part of the road to knowledge of God. To become aware of God the individual must enter the darkness within him, the unexplored hinterland of the personality' (Bryant, 1983).

This is territory that many so-called 'Bible-believing' Christians avoid. Not only does it mean facing the remaining remnants of childhood self-absorption and preoccupation with meeting the needs of oneself, it also involves becoming aware of some of the powerful hidden forces of unacknowledged and unfamiliar aggression, hatred and destructiveness and the powerful drives of sex. None of this makes for a comfortable life! On occasion, Christians who are afraid of this dark, shadow side of themselves take Bible words and use them to avoid facing the reality of what they themselves are really like under the outer respectable mask they wear most of the time. Words like the following are used: 'Whatever is honourable, just, pure, lovely, gracious, if there is any excellence, if there is anything worthy of praise, think about these things' (Philippians 4.8). A deduction is made by some people (and is sometimes given the authoritative prefix 'the Bible teaches') that not only are such wholesome things to fill the thoughts of the Christian, but also that their opposites are to be denied a place in the devout Christian's mind. I have noticed that, on occasion, a Christian will grab such Bible words and use them as a reason for failing to deal with some of the uglier aspects of themselves.

RECONCILING OPPOSITES

There is an important first step that must be taken in seeking to bring one area of ourselves into proximity with another that is in conflict with it. This involves facing, coming to terms with, and perhaps even embracing, that which Jung calls our 'personal shadow'. This involves doing something that is the opposite of that taught in some church circles. It is sometimes taught that we should 'cast out', 'get rid of', 'exorcise' (or whatever term is used) those 'nasties' within that disquiet us. In doing this, we deprive ourselves of something that can, surprisingly, be the making of us, give us a hidden strength, and turn out to be something very important without which we are the poorer. If we are to become complete, whole, full Christians, then both the 'nice' and the 'nasty' need to jostle within us – like the shade and light that are both indispensable parts of a painting and held close together within the picture's frame. The first step towards 'integration' is similar in many ways to the *metanoia*, the change of heart, with which an unbeliever faces up to himself and turns to Christ with what he is. Self-awareness has then begun and, hopefully, continues.

THE VALUE OF SYMBOLS

However, while self-knowledge is the ingredient vital for bringing about inner change, it is as impotent as dried yeast as long as it remains in a paper packet, isolated from the sugar, warmth and moisture that allow fermentation to occur. It is Jesus Christ, a living symbol, who can be the agent through which a Christian's fermentation or transformation occurs. In Jungian thought, the power that is able to bring order out of inner confusion and chaos is the power of the symbol. Some of us from Protestant backgrounds flinch at any mention of symbols in religion. In Sunday school we were taught that we

98   *Good Enough For God*

had descended from the Reformers, that their fight against Roman Catholicism was our fight, that we are to be true to our forefathers and flee from anything that might lead us towards Rome. Lumped under that fearsome 'anything', for some of us from certain Protestant traditions, are the dreaded (or so we were taught as children) faith-destroying 'rituals' and 'symbols'. In their enthusiasm to ensure that we understood that we were saved by Christ's death on the Cross, by this and this alone, and that we could not *earn* salvation by being 'good' or by meeting certain requirements of the Church (saying 'Hail Mary's', genuflecting before the altar, making a pilgrimage to Rome, being blessed by the Pope and so on), some of our teachers powerfully communicated that symbols and rituals could be mistaken for the 'real thing' and could lead us so astray that we lost our eternal salvation. This has meant that some of us have been so busy fearing and running away from the symbolic that we have missed out on the transforming power some religious symbols could have in our lives. We may also have failed to understand that a symbol has an 'as if' label attached to it – so that when we allow the symbol of, say, a lion to work deeply inside us, it is as if a lion enters us and we discover more courage in our quaking hearts than we would have believed possible. Bryant puts it this way: 'There is a gulf between my rational will and my archetypal instincts, between my head and my heart. This gulf is bridged by the living symbol' (Bryant, 1983).

Symbols are cross-cultural, international and transcend linguistic barriers. They belong in two different places at the same time. A symbol is there in our external daily lives but it also has a niche in the inner world of our unconscious. We can think about a symbol, sit and enjoy and relish it or hate and fear it, contemplate its beauty or horror, play with it in our imagination, listen to its music, try to probe its depths, try to strip it to its core to discover its many-layered meanings or see what ideas and thoughts connect to it in our minds. We can open ourselves wide to try to sense the deepest meaning it holds for us and yet it is impossible to completely grasp and understand a symbol. We can never exhaust all that is contained in a symbol for 'it is rooted in the unconscious and draws its power from the archetypal energies that it activates within us. . . . There is a reservoir of psychic energy within men and women which cannot be tapped by will-power alone. Only the living symbol can lead it out and make it available to the conscious personality' (Bryant, 1983).

Carl Jung describes symbols as being like huge turbine engines that transform the force of the water pouring over the Niagara Falls into electric power, light and heat. In similar ways, Bryant suggests that 'the living symbol by focusing the imagination releases the instinctual archetypal energy and emotion and so empowers action. Religion is powerful through its symbols, through images and figures, personal and impersonal, that stir men and women to their depths. For the living symbol liberates the spiritual energy latent within and guides it into the service of the values which religion upholds' (Bryant, 1983).

HUMAN NATURE AND SIN

Yet one fact about being human still remains inescapably clear. When it comes to seeking to live as we long to live, we are guaranteed a life of conflict as well as a life of peace. We live with inner tension threatening to tear apart our very selves – the tension existing between our reality and the ideals that most of us set before ourselves. Failure to attain these ideals leaves us conscious that we are not what we often set out to be. It is at these moments, when our failure stabs us keenly, that words in certain hymns (talking about 'the peace and contentment and freedom from strife we have in Christ') rub salt into our inner wounds. We discover that the process of sanctification is often as painful to our souls as the sharp grit that wounds the flesh of a pearl-producing oyster. It also takes time; our sanctification is not instantaneous.

Meanwhile, we are stuck with ourselves. The apostle Paul likes the situation no more than we do and bursts out with his words of despair, 'I know that nothing good dwells within me, that is, in my flesh. I can will what is right, but I cannot do it.

For I do not do the good I want, but the evil I do not want is what I do. Now if I do what I do not want, it is no longer I that do it, but sin which dwells within me' (Romans 7.18–20).

To some psychologists, this thing called 'sin', about which Paul writes, appears to be similar, if not identical to, the Jungian aspect of the personality called the 'shadow'. Of both sin and of the shadow can be said: 'it acts like a sub-personality gathering to itself despised and rejected elements inconsistent with the individual's ideal; and is liable to push itself into the driving seat of the personality and take temporary control' (Bryant, 1983).

Paul not only cries out in despair but chooses this moment in time to bring its opposite, hope, into view and hold the two close together. He says, 'Wretched man that I am! Who will deliver me from this body of death? Thanks be to God through Jesus Christ our Lord!' (Romans 7.24, 25). Paul was able to speak with the authoritative voice of experience, for at his conversion on the road to Damascus, opposites – 'both the despised and rejected elements in his personality and the strong ethical ideals which had led him to their rejection' (Bryant, 1983) – were welded together in such light that he was blinded by its brightness. 'Allegiance to Christ and trust in him brought unity in place of division and peace after conflict. He experienced a flooding of love, joy and peace which he ascribes sometimes to the Holy Spirit, and sometimes to Christ dwelling in him' (Bryant, 1983). His being delivered from 'this body of death' was a powerful metaphor that he used to point to the close identification Christians have with the weakness and vulnerability of the Jesus who was crucified, from which its opposite – the power of the resurrection – bursts into life.

ACHIEVING LASTING CHANGE

Bryant reminds us that change is not usually so dramatically instantaneous – old habits die hard, old thought patterns take time to be replaced with new ones. But 'as an individual learns step-by-step to trust more and more the outcast

elements of his personality to the power of Christ, once despised and rejected but now endowed with absolute authority,
these elements tend to change their character until eventually, not without alarms and apparent relapses, they become
his allies rather than his enemies; they play a necessary part in
his progress on the road to self-fulfilment' (Bryant, 1983).

Sandra discovered that understanding herself and the way
childhood had affected her meant that she brought together
two very different parts of herself. With her head she understood how she had become the person she was and knew that
there were certain things she wanted to change. Her heart
also understood and felt compassion for the little girl she had
been who had never had enough of her busy mother's undivided attention. Her compassion for that child, and her
understanding that it was this deprivation that led her to steal,
helped her to love that child. She became aware not only of
her love for her mother, but also of her anger with her mother,
who had not been able to give her enough. Sandra also discovered in God a parent who loved her deeply – a parent she
could experience as one who loved her tenderly, wanted to
spend time with her and saw her as very special. She changed,
but how she changed cannot be reduced to a simple formula.
Suffice it to say that something transforming occurred. She
sees herself as being as different now to then as a butterfly is
to a caterpillar. She has learned in prayer how to 'hold the
mind in the heart' (Bryant, 1983).

10

Cross and Crossroad

Temptation is what distracts us, beguiles us or bullies us off the path. Temptation is what makes real life different from the world of our dreams. We dream a world which is wax under the moulding of our ambitions or of our aspirations; we meet a world which faces us with trials we have not the character to surmount, and with seductions we have not the virtue to resist.

(Farrer, 1970)

CYRIL'S STORY

There were times when Cyril felt that, no matter what he did or said, he was doomed not to get it right. No matter how or what he was, he could never please everyone nor be what everyone else seemed to expect him to be. Above all, he longed to be the kind of man who was satisfying to God, to be a man who was 'holy', and he often found that he was measuring his probable acceptability to God and his apparent 'attained degree of holiness' by the yardstick of what his Christian friends thought about certain things. His vague, not thought through assumption was that if any group of people knew what God wanted from people, then that group was bound to be made up of sincere Christians like his friends.

This posed problems. On the one hand, these friends implied that for him, as for all Christians, certain things lurked in the shadows of life that would seduce and distract him away from his aim of being holy and hinder him from 'walking in God's pathway'. But, on the other hand, it was the 'not doing' of some of these 'dubious' things that, confusingly, impaired his witness as a Christian and he was clear that 'being a good witness' was something expected of all whole-hearted followers of Christ.

Cyril was a hospital doctor, and the group of doctors who worked together on certain wards would go to the pub once a week with the Consultant for a couple of hours, to chat, unburden themselves and have a good laugh or cry with one another once the beer had loosened their inhibitions. This was the time for the doctors to relate to each other as human beings, to take off their medical masks, and it was the time when it would have seemed very natural for Cyril to talk about his faith. However, he had been taught since he was a child that drinking was sinful and would set him on a downward pathway leading away from holy living. He had been warned that he should be wary of going into pubs for (according to his parents and others whose opinions he valued) they were frequented by dangerous people who would undermine his faith. Cyril knew the words in the Bible 'Be ye holy for I am holy!' and 'Come out from among them and be ye separate!' On the strength of these words and on the advice of his 'keenest' church friends, he allowed himself to stick out like a sore thumb and refused the drinks and hours of friendship his colleagues offered him, choosing instead to sit alone in the hospital library reading a medical journal. This meant that he was never present when his work peers talked about themselves and their lives, he never shared himself with them and they regarded him as a stuck-up 'holy Joe' who thought he was superior to the rest of humanity. The command that Christians are to be 'holy' does not necessarily imply that Christians have to set themselves on a pinnacle of pious isolation above the world of ordinary living and perceive it as being full of potentially dangerous, contaminating people and ideas.

SOME THOUGHTS ON HOLINESS

Crabb's discussion of the word 'holy' in his dictionary of English synonyms offers some pertinent comments, giving a different perspective on the subject. He says that '*holiness*, from Anglo-Saxon *halig*, allied to *hal*, whole and health, has altogether acquired a Christian signification; it respects the life and temper of a Christian. *Sanctity*, based on the Latin *sanctus*, holy, has merely a moral signification, which it derives from the *sanction* of human authority' (Crabb, 1966). He then goes on to explain the difference between holiness and sanctity, stating that '*holiness* is to the mind of man what *sanctity* is to his exterior, with this difference, that *holiness* to a certain degree ought to belong to every man professing Christianity; but *sanctity*, as it lies in the manners, the outward garb, and deportment is becoming only to certain persons and at certain times. *Holiness* is a thing not to be effected; but *sanctity*, consisting in externals, is from its very nature exposed to falsehood. It becomes those who fill a sacred office, but no others' (Crabb, 1966).

I am intrigued to discover that holiness, according to Crabb, is about wholeness and health. Cyril, and others like him, do not appear to me to be healthy, whole or mature individuals. They seem to be living in a frightening no man's land, in a state of siege, protecting themselves from unknown dangers in an environment that others see as the normal world of daily life. At times, it seems as if the likes of Cyril have hammered a wedge between certain aspects of themselves, splitting them apart, and are trying to keep these aspects as far apart as possible. In particular, the undesirable and shameful aspects of the self are banished from consciousness when possible. Some Christians call these undesirables 'evil spirits' and then go through some kind of process by which the undesirable is 'cast out'. However, I believe that an essential part of wholeness, of health, holiness, is the bringing together closely inside us of these widely separated aspects of ourselves rather than attempting (with varying degrees of success or failure) to get rid of them. I believe that the achievement of wholeness and of holiness involves a continuous movement in the direction of bringing opposites closer together, rather than dispersing them, getting rid of them or rigidly holding them as far apart as possible. This moving towards wholeness is also called 'individuation'.

THE SYMBOLISM OF THE CROSS

Modern Jungian analyst Joseph Redfearn points out that Carl Jung saw wholeness as being implicit in the 'tremendous tension of opposites paradoxically at one, as in the cross, their most powerful symbol' (Redfearn, 1993). He suggests that 'the image of opposing elements meeting, with the liberation or absorption of immense quantities of energy, good or bad, is so all-pervasive that it is hardly possible to exaggerate its psychological importance' (Redfearn, 1993). He goes on to link this idea with Christianity and claims, of the power of opposites meeting, that 'this is the energy underlying . . . the illuminating, shattering properties of the God image, and this is the energy underlying the individuation process. One symbol, that of the cross, "contains" the most cruel, sadistic torture, given and received, and sublime self-sacrifice and redemption' (Redfearn, 1993).

I am used to seeing in the cross a symbol of salvation, redemption and atonement, and of trying to understand that Jesus Christ, God's holy One, was 'made sin' for us so that we might become holy. I am used to thinking of this in terms of a transaction in which Christ was substituted for me on the cross (for the reality – according to this line of thought – was that it *was* me who needed to be put to death) and then, by his death, my sins were wiped away and so I no longer needed to experience divine punishment. In my teens, I learned that something called 'justification' occurred so that, at the moment when I trusted Christ as my Saviour, it was just as if I had never sinned. I got hold of the idea that once this had happened I had, by my acceptance of salvation, become one of God's 'holy people'. But I was then left with the problem that although my life might have been regarded by others as being fairly good, I knew in my heart of hearts that it was not all that good and it was probably not 'holy'. And so I have struggled with trying to understand what other meanings the cross and concepts of holiness might contain.

Theatre director, writer and non-stipendiary Anglican clergyman James Roose-Evans has explored some of the meanings contained in the symbolism of the cross. He suggests that for 'many Christians the sign of the cross has become a perfunctory gesture, even verging on mindless superstition. And yet, if we open ourselves to its deeper meaning it can, once again, come alive, and be seen not only as the central symbol of Christianity but a profound archetype for everyone, for this crossroads sign, this meeting-of-the-opposites, is to be found in many cultures and throughout history' (Roose-Evans, 1994). Having described how to centre-down and inwardly concentrate and focus on the symbolism of the cross, and thus discover 'the kingdom of God within', he adds further discoveries that are open to us. 'It is a sign, and to cross is to signify. Those who cannot write their own names are asked to sign with a cross. It is the primordial signature' (Roose-Evans, 1994).

A Jungian analyst, Bani Shorter, sheds further light when she points out that 'crossings and crossroads are of deep symbolic meaning in life. It was Hermes, the Messenger of the Gods, who was guardian of the crossroads in ancient Greece. There, where one is challenged by change of direction and choice, one encounters one's god, and signifies as oneself and to oneself but also in relation to that Other' (Shorter, 1989). Indeed, it is at the cross of Jesus Christ that many of us Christians encounter our God.

Roose-Evans links places where paths and lines cross to Christ's cross and sees how 'the vertical line of God and infinity cuts through the horizontal line of mankind and time, creating a tension of opposites. And it is at the centre of this tension that each of us has to learn how to live, uniting in each of us all opposites: male/female, dark/light, reason/intuition, God/human, sacred/secular' (Roose-Evans, 1994).

THE IMPORTANCE OF OTHER SYMBOLS

We are familiar with biblical teaching that 'Christ is our peace' and I see this not in terms of our passively using Christ as a way of covering up the inner state of affairs, of bolstering our denying and repressive defences, but, rather, as actively working within us to own and integrate some of our conflicting opposites. Many of us slip into the habit of using prayer and of using Jesus Christ as a kind of soothing cough syrup to quell the irritation of whatever inner conflict is causing us discomfort. We pray, are comforted and may thus manage to 'magic away' our feelings of discomfort. I am wary of this technique. I see it as misusing prayer and making it the equivalent of putting a dummy into a crying baby's mouth. It is reasonable sometimes, when we are upset and need immediate comfort, to find pacifiers for ourselves as a temporary measure, but, in the long term, it is important that we try to deal with the root issue.

As a doctor, I know that usually it is in the best interests of an individual with a chronic cough for whatever has led to the chest discomfort (sputum, lung secretions, infection, foreign bodies) to be allowed to cause discomfort so that it will eventually be coughed out. If this does not happen, it may settle and lead to pneumonia. In the same way, I believe that our inner conflicts are best handled by allowing them to irritate, surface painfully and be exposed to the light of conscious awareness. In this way, we begin to find healing, wholeness and integration.

I believe that this is one of the ways in which Jesus Christ can have a transforming effect on the lives of Christians. Carl Jung was clear about the importance of Christ as a symbol in some peoples' quest for wholeness and explains that 'looked at from the psychological standpoint, Christ, as the Original Man . . . represents a totality which surpasses and includes ordinary man, and which corresponds to the total personality that transcends consciousness. We have called this personality the "self"' (Jung, 1958). Jung's statement reminds me of the description of the transcendent goal for which Christians aim as being to 'attain to the unity of the faith and of the knowledge of the Son of God, to mature manhood, to the measure of the stature of the fullness of Christ' (Ephesians 4.13).

For Jung, the events of the life of Christ were paradigms for the process of self-realization. He says, 'The drama of the archetypal life of Christ describes in symbolic images the events in the conscious life – as well as life that transcends consciousness – of a man who has been transformed by his higher destiny' (Jacobi, 1959). And symbols are extremely powerful for, like a certain beer, they reach parts of us that nothing else reaches. This happens because symbols influence every function we possess.

When I was working as a hospital chaplain, with people facing crises, I discovered that while my words and my touch were valuable, it was often the use of symbols that touched people at a deep level of themselves and seemed to give them something they could not receive in any other way. For one woman who had breast cancer that had spread to other parts of her body, it was the flowers embroidered on my sweater that gave her hope of life – if not of life in this world, then of something that would go on after she had died – something into which she would blossom and flower.

For another woman dying of cancer, it was the Southend-on-Sea she had visited for childhood holidays and for her honeymoon that symbolized the place she longed to go to once she was released from her pain-racked body. A few days before she died, she whispered to me, 'I'm going to that other Southend quite soon, you know', and I could not stop my tears, for her use of symbolic language moved me profoundly.

Other patients and their relatives used more common symbols, like the cross or a rosary. Mark Searle comments that 'the existence of community rituals, which express common beliefs in common symbols and common disciplines, serves to assure the person-in-crisis that what he or she is going through is not only meaningful, but also good; and not only good, but necessary for the well-being both of themselves and of the whole community' (Searle, 1980).

Another experienced priest, Raymond Studzinski, writing about mid-life, shares his experience of how 'religious symbols help to draw order out of the chaos people may experience at mid-life. They are powerful unifiers, drawing into a whole one's fragmented self and life' (Studzinski, 1985). He sees the mid-life transition stage as being 'a passage from an old way of ordering life, through a chaotic period when the old order breaks down, to a new order in which polarities are more adequately balanced and reconciled' (Studzinski, 1985). His experience is that 'Christian rituals, such as the Eucharist, can speak effectively and energetically . . . The cross and the paschal event can illuminate the dying and rising which mid-life entails' (Studzinski, 1985). He finds that at this time of life, 'there is an openness to symbols especially when one's established structures are left behind in the mid-life quest for better structures. Ritual and symbols help a person to name this experience of chaos and channel energy into new ways of relating to the self and to the world' (Studzinski, 1985).

Cyril was trapped in a world of concrete absolutes so he believed it when he was told 'alcohol is bad and will lead you away from God's holy pathway'. He therefore sought to be 'holy' by avoiding anything that might contaminate him. This meant that he was so separate from his colleagues that he was unable to share what he had to offer and was unable to receive from them their gifts. Here was a man who, week by week, shared the broken Body and Blood of his Lord at the Communion service in his church and yet failed to understand how the sharing of wine can be a symbol of the sharing of one's life with others. In his *concrete* understanding he had missed *symbolic* meaning, and had symbolically communicated that his life and those of his colleagues were not to intermingle. Perhaps they felt that in his eyes their life's blood contained a deadly virus that would destroy his spiritual immune system, for his fear of being contaminated by them was so great!

If holiness has more to do with wholeness than it has to do with avoiding contamination, and inner wholeness can be facilitated by symbols, then it behoves Christians to think deeply and carefully about the possible meanings lying behind and under situations and events in their lives. Holiness is then seen in terms of being more wholly the person you are. I think that Joyce Grenfell would have understood what I am trying to say. She wrote, 'I think what I am doing is losing Joyce Grenfell and finding out the person God made. The older you get the more you realize that happiness is losing your false sense of what you are, your false self. What was that lovely quotation: "Become what you are!" Well, that interpreted means become what your true potential is, your spiritual wholeness' (source unknown).

As Socrates said, 'It is the unexamined, the unloved life that is not worth living'.

11

Wholly Holy

In the deep jungles of Africa, a traveller was making a long trek. Coolies had been engaged from a tribe to carry the loads. The first day they marched rapidly and went far. The traveller had high hopes of a speedy journey. But the second morning these jungle tribesmen refused to move. On enquiry as to the reason for this strange behaviour, the traveller was informed that they had gone too fast the first day, and they were now waiting for their souls to catch up with their bodies.

(Cowman, 1939)

MARY'S STORY

I listened to Mary's story with growing fascination. Her eyes glowed and her face flushed warmly while she tried to share her experience with me. She, like an African jungle tribesman who has travelled, fleet-footed, at high speed across a desert, was pausing for lengthy reflection to allow her soul time and space to catch up with her body. But it was nearly impossible for Mary's mind to catch up with, grasp and articulate her experience. It seemed almost impossible and quite beyond her to find words able and adequate to describe her encounter with God.

She told me about a remote, distant God who came as an immediate presence and who fused with her innermost essence in a deathly single, yet multiple, burning, living union. The words of a popular hymnwriter sum up, in a nutshell, what she was trying to share, 'tis mystery all, the immortal dies' ('Amazing Grace', John Newton).

DESCRIBING ENCOUNTERS WITH THE HOLY

There are moments when it is impossible to describe our encounters with the holy, for mystery defies the definition required by rational minds. Rudolph Otto suggested using the words 'numen' and 'numinous' to describe this definitive and peculiar quality of the religious, which he wrote of as being overwhelming and fascinating mystery. It is encountered in different religions and in different kinds of ecstatic experiences and is not the unique property of Judaeo-Christian believers.

A common way of using the word 'holy' implies that something is present which consists of a special essence. This is seen in phrases like 'treading on holy ground', 'holy smoke!' and 'his holiness'. These expressions carry the implication that something out of the ordinary is being encountered, which not only is connected with the religious but also usually involves either a benign or a malevolent, non-human presence. This 'presence' tends to assume larger-than-life proportions, has an over-the-top quality to it, is diffuse, overwhelming and indefinable and yet provides 'order, orientation, life, sustenance and meaning to existence in space and time, a dimension of "otherness", primal and foundational, upon which everything in creation depends, yet which is not subject to human manipulation or control' (Richardson and Bowden, 1983).

Defining 'holiness' requires a mobile and malleable mind, for holiness refuses to be bound within simple, clear-cut limits. Holiness is something that is far more universal than we tend to realize. In the words of a theologian, 'It is not a quality that by contrast brands the creaturely as profane and unclean, or that differentiates between sacred and secular, whether in times, places, or states of life. For the hour has come when the whole of creation is now God's holy place and sphere of action (Psalm 24.3; John 4.21)' (Macquarrie and Childress, 1986). Holiness is inwardly transforming, change-producing, and enables people to recognize 'what is good and acceptable and perfect' (Romans 12.1,2). It entails a horror of moral defilement (2 Corinthians 7.1) and requires a complete break with one's former state of death, darkness and sin (1 Corinthians 6.9–11; Macquarrie and Childress, 1986). God's people reflect God's holiness and the result may be 'a consecration of power in the service of love. It combines the mystery of holy election with that of God's will to save all people (1 Timothy 2.4); and God's moral requirements for his holy ones are no set of voluntarist injunctions, but a revelation of his own concern for universal justice' (Macquarrie and Childress, 1986).

It is hard to take all this in. As I try to imagine what it might mean, I find that I am caught up in a sense of deep awe, of profound awareness of this 'other'. This other is there at times as a fearful inner presence of burning white light or as a solid nugget of pure gold deep within or as indefinable warm comfort. This other is both very close and very distant, both immanent while simultaneously being transcendent. I have also experienced the numinous in those rare moments when extreme opposites like intense love and intense hatred have been blended and fused internally, as if two separate metal rods of white-hot iron are being united and beaten into shape by some unseen blacksmith on the fiery anvil of my heart. At moments like these, I am able to sense the overwhelming nature of holiness that is communicated in words like 'You shall therefore be holy, for I am holy' (Leviticus 11.45), 'Holy, holy, holy is the Lord of hosts . . . the whole earth is full of his glory . . . Woe is me! for I am lost; for I am a man of unclean lips; for mine eyes have seen the King, the Lord of hosts' (Isaiah 6.3, 5).

HOW ARE WE TO BECOME HOLY?

Academic discussions about the nature of holiness are drowned at such times, they seem irrelevant and may become lost in the overwhelmingly awesome nature of contemplating the holy one himself. God's people not only experience the numinous but are called to lead a life of holiness and goodness. A professor of theology puts it this way: 'The relation of the holy to morality becomes explicit, not as if morality is added to the *numinous*, but because holiness includes morality although it is more than morality, and because the "lostness" of the prophet, mentioned immediately afterwards, includes unworthiness' (Richardson and Bowden, 1983). I am left out of breath, as if I have run a marathon through amazing country and been unable to take in the immensity and the detail of the landscape through which I have travelled.

Holiness brings a standard to bear on practical daily living that may seem unattainable to most of us for, in the Judaeo-Christian ethical tradition, holiness is, first and foremost, a divine attribute, indicating a radical otherness about God's inner world. How can we ever hope to reach the kind of Godlikeness to which it seems we are called to aspire? We fall down and worship in awed reverence before the supreme majesty and purity of the 'numinous', before that presence which Tillich calls 'the divine ground of our being' (Macquarrie and Childress, 1986). How then, we may wonder, could we possibly have the audacity or muster enough courage to hope or to presume that we, mere human beings, could mirror qualities belonging to such a holy one. It seems beyond us. We observe qualities we could aim for in the life of Jesus Christ but continually fall short of the mark when we try to do so. In the words of a theologian, 'For Christians, holiness is supremely manifest in the mystery of Jesus Christ, in whose life, teaching, death and resurrection the powers of righteousness and love of God's kingdom are already present. Everything that sustains and redeems as well as everything that cleanses and purifies and fulfils, that empowers faith, hope and love, is understood in relation to the holiness manifest in Jesus Christ' (Richardson and Bowden, 1983).

And so, as the *New Dictionary of Christian Ethics* points out, we find in the New Testament that Jesus 'sanctified' himself to his 'holy' father, so that his followers might be made holy in the truth of his word and might be kept safe in the world (John 17.11, 15–19). The Church is thus made up of people who have been sanctified (made holy) through Jesus' dedication of himself (1 Corinthians 1.2), people who were especially selected years before they were born to be those who would be washed clean and carefully ironed so that no creases spoiled their holy, spotless fabric (Ephesians 1.4; 5.25–27). These people are a chosen race, the 'holy nation' that was foreshadowed in Israel, and are called by the holy God to be holy in all aspects of their lives (1 Peter 1.15, 16; 2.9; Ephesians 5.3). They have been chosen, selected and singled out rather than set apart and are to aim at attaining 'righteousness for sanctification' (Romans 6.19). In this way, they live out the 'holiness and righteousness' promised a long time ago by God (Luke 1.75). This is personified in Jesus, who was God's 'holy and righteous One' (Acts 3.14), which is now apparent in the lives of God's children – because of his renewal of creation in his own likeness 'in true righteousness and holiness' (Ephesians 4.23, 24). For each Christian, holiness can be seen as something that weaves together three different-coloured threads – one signifying divine initiative or election, another signifying distinctiveness from all that is not of God and the third denoting dedication to God's holy purposes (adapted from Macquarrie and Childress, 1986).

This all sounds too good to be true. It seems unattainable – like a glorious night filled with amazing dreams from which we know we must wake, realizing that common sense is true and that we are not like this and never shall be. I take comfort from Thomas Aquinas' statement that 'grace is nothing else than a beginning of glory in us'. It is as if the seed of glory has been sown in our hearts that will, in God's time and place, blossom and fruit.

HOLINESS AND FREE WILL

A question then arises. If a seed has been sown that will inevitably develop and mature into ripe fruit, is there anything we ought to do to cultivate and fertilize it? Are we to do anything other than sit under a sunshade, smiling benignly at our plot of land? Are we free to let our lives run riot, possibly turning into dissolute, weed-filled, chaotic messes? Can we then expect God to clear out all this accumulated rubbish

with heavenly bulldozers and dumper trucks? Is it legitimate
for us to adopt an attitude like 'The worse the mess, the more
seeds of grace will have to be sown to utilize the rubbish, and
so the end result will be a bumper crop of fruit. So, QED, let
things go to rack and ruin as that way we benefit more'? The
apostle Paul countered such suggestions with his question
'Are we to continue in sin that grace may abound?' And with
his answer, 'By no means! How can we who died to sin still
live in it?' (Romans 6.1, 2)

Controversy has raged in the Church down the ages as to
whether or not people have an innate capacity to make good
choices and live holy lives or whether prior to birth they have
been flawed so fatally that nothing but God's grace can make
anything good possible. The controversy is further complicated
by questions relating to those whom God has chosen to be the
people he elects to transform through his grace. Are these
potentially to be elected individuals able to *resist* God's selection process or is God's election and choice of them irresistible?
Once chosen and elected by God, is anyone really free to say,
'Yes, I'll go along with this!' or 'No, I don't want it!'?

This came to a head in debates in the early Church between Pelagius, a British monk, and Augustine of Hippo.
Pelagius 'wanted all Christians to be dedicated to an austere
struggle with mediocrity, an arduous quest for perfection'
(McManners, 1993). Henry Chadwick, a historian, explains
that Pelagius was particularly 'alarmed when a bishop had
quoted in his hearing a prayer from Augustine's *Confessions*:
"Thou commandedst continence; grant what thou com-
mandest and command what thou wilt". The use made of
these words seemed to Pelagius to undermine moral responsibility and to preach cheap grace' (Chadwick, 1967). It
seemed obvious to Pelagius that people had to be free to
make their own choices so that they could then be account-
able to God. If this were not so, they would then be mere
marionettes whose strings God pulled, making them mind-
lessly do exactly what he wanted. Pelagius was convinced
that sin does not affect the power of the human will to make
decisions and carry out actions an individual chooses.

As far as Augustine was concerned, the freedom the New Testament taught us about was far more than mere academic theory – it was something alive and powerful. For him, *true* New Testament freedom involved being free enough 'to will what you would do if you willed it' (Burnaby, 1966). His attitude was that, if left to its own devices, the human will would inevitably lead someone into sin, for, in its natural state, it was 'diseased, weakened, prone to evil' (Burnaby, 1966). As he saw it, 'the work of grace is to heal and restore the will, by imparting to it that delight in righteousness without which the knowledge of what is right must be ineffective. And nothing can make righteousness delightful to us but the love of God which we can never create in ourselves; for the love of God is God's gift of himself, given by and with the presence of the Holy Spirit in our hearts (Romans 5.5)' (Burnaby, 1966).

This was debated vigorously by early theologians from Jerome through to Augustine. 'From these debates crystallized, eventually, the doctrine of grace and merit, finally in a form which fell short both of the teaching of Pelagius and of the extreme views (ruthless predestination, divine election irrespective of human merits) propounded by Augustine in his old age' (McManners, 1993).

The apostle Paul had earlier grappled with this conflict. He wrote, confusingly, that people were to 'work out your own salvation for it is God that worketh in you' (Philippians 2.12, 13). In John Burnaby's words, 'Between Pelagius and Augustine, the two arms of Paul's paradox were torn apart. Pelagius carried off the first – "work out your own salvation" – and Augustine the second – "it is God that worketh in you". In Augustine's religion, Christian freedom is the willing service inspired by life. In his theology, it is grace that makes us willing instead of unwilling . . . the grace of God makes possible the answer of faith for which it calls, but it does not compel. Grace *cannot* compel, it must be the activity of love; for love and compulsion are incompatible' (Burnaby, 1966).

Living a holy life, becoming increasingly whole, moving towards integration, becoming more and more the people we truly are, finding healing, becoming more Christlike and loving ourselves and others, are things we work towards and which are worked within us. As we live, as we love and as we work, we need, in the words of a chorus from my childhood, to 'take time to be holy', for allowing our souls to catch up with our bodies means creating the space in our lives in which the seeds of grace sown within can be nurtured to fruition.

A FINAL THOUGHT

As I look back over some of the territory explored in this book, I am increasingly aware that, from my perspective, many Christian beliefs and many of the insights of psychology blend together and enhance each other. John Calvin wrote, 'it is manifest that man will never obtain a perfect knowledge concerning himself, *unless* he has first beheld God's countenance and then descends from his look to the contemplation of self' (Hurding, 1985).

Bibliography

Astor, James, and Fordham, Michael, *Innovations in Analytical Psychology* (Routledge, 1995)

Atkinson, David, and Field, David (eds), *New Dictionary of Christian Ethics and Pastoral Theology* (IVP, 1995)

Augustine of Hippo, *Confessions* (Penguin, 1961)

Barclay, William, *The Daily Study Bible*, Matthew, Vol. 1 (St Andrew Press, 1978)

Bettelheim, Bruno, *Freud and Man's Soul* (Penguin, 1991)

Bion, W. R., *Brazilian Lectures 1* (Rio de Janeiro, Imago Editora, 1974)

Bowen, Elizabeth, *Death of the Heart* (Penguin, 1990)

Bryant, Christopher, *Jung and the Christian Way* (DLT, 1983)

Burnaby, John, *Christian Words and Christian Meanings* (Hodder and Stoughton, 1966)

Campbell, Alastair V. (ed.), *A Dictionary of Pastoral Care* (SPCK, 1987)

Chadwick, Henry, *The Early Church* (Pelican, 1967)

Coate, Mary Anne, *Clergy Stress* (SPCK, 1989)

Collins English Dictionary (Collins, 1988)

Cowman, Lettie, *Springs in the Valley* (Grand Rapids, Zondervan, 1939)

Crabb's English Synonyms (Routledge, 1966)

Eliot, T. S., *Collected Poems 1909–1962* (Faber and Faber, 1974)

Farrer, Austin, *A Celebration of Faith* (Hodder, 1970)

Fordham, Frieda, *An Introduction to Jung's Psychology* (Penguin, 1953)

Fordham, Michael, *The Objective Psyche* (Routledge, 1958)

Freud, Anna, *The Ego and Mechanisms of Defence* (Hogarth, 1968)

Freud, Sigmund, *The Future of an Illusion* (Liveright, 1953)

Freud, Sigmund, Strachey, James, (ed.), *Standard Edition*, Vol. 18 (Hogarth Press, 1921)

Gittings, Robert, *John Keats by 1968* (Penguin, 1979)

Gordon, Rosemary, *Dying and Creating* (Library of Analytical Psychology, Vol. 4, 1978)

Grant, Harold, Thompson, Magdala, and Clarke, Thomas, *From Image to Likeness* (Paulist Press, 1983)

Guthrie, Donald, *New Testament Theology* (IVP, 1981)

Harding, Esther, Foreword by C. G. Jung in *Woman's Mysteries* (New York, 1955)

Hurding, Roger, quoting John Calvin in *Roots and Shoots* (Hodder and Stoughton, 1985)

Jacobi, Jolande, *Complex-Archetype-Symbol in the Psychology of C. G. Jung* (Bollingen Series, Pantheon Books, 1959)

Jung, C. G., *The Archetypes and the Collective Unconscious* (Routledge, 1992)

Jung, C. G., *Collected Works*, Vol. 6 (Routledge, 1978)

Jung, C. G., *Collected Works*, Vol. 8 (Routledge, 1978)

Jung, C. G., *Psychological Types* (Routledge, 1989)

Jung, Carl, *Psychology and Religion: West and East* (Bollingen Series, Pantheon Books, 1958)

Jung, Carl, *Psychology and Religion: West and East* (Routledge, 1969)

Klein, Josephine, *Our Need for Others and its Root in Infancy* (Routledge, 1987)

Laplanche, J., and Pontialis, J. B., *The Language of Psychoanalysis* (Karnac Books, 1988)

Lawrence, D. H., *The Collected Poems* (Viking, 1964)

McManners, John, (ed.) *The Oxford History of Christianity* (Oxford, 1993)

Macquarrie, John, and Childress, James, (eds) *A New Dictionary of Christian Ethics* (SCM, 1986)

Molon, Phil, *The Fragile Self* (Whurr Publishers, 1993)

Neumann, Erich, *The Origins and History of Consciousness* (Karnac, 1989)

O'Connor, Elizabeth, quoted by Kelsey, Morton, in *Transcend* (Crossroad, 1986)

Parsons, Gerald, *Religion in Victorian Britain, Vol. 2: Controversies* (Open University, 1988)

Redfearn, Joseph, *My Self, My Many Selves* (Academic Press, 1993)

Redfearn, Joseph, *The Exploding Self* (Chiron, 1992)

Richardson, Alan, and Bowden, John, (eds), *A New Dictionary of Christian Theology* (SCM, 1983)

Roose-Evans, James, *Passages of the Soul* (Element, 1994)

Samuels, Andrew, Shorter, Bani, and Plaut, Fred, *A Critical Dictionary of Jungian Analysis* (Routledge, 1992)

Schwartz-Salant, Nathan, *Narcissism and Character Transformation* (Inner City Books, 1982)

Searle, Mark, 'The Journey of Conversion' (Worship, 54, 1980)

Shannon, Richard, *The Peacock and the Phoenix*

Shorter, Bani, *If Ritual Dies* (Guild of Pastoral Psychology, Lecture 231, 1989)

Studzinski, Raymond, *Spiritual Direction and Midlife Development* (Loyola University, 1985)

Symington, Neville, *The Analytic Experience* (Free Association Books, 1986)

Ulanov, Ann and Barry, *Primary Speech* (SCM Press, 1985)

Wandor, Michelene, *Gardens of Eden* (Journeyman Press/Play Books, 1984)

Winnicott, D. W., *Playing and Reality* (Penguin, 1971)

Woman Alive (1994)

Wright Beare, Francis, *The Gospel According to Matthew* (Basil Blackwell, 1981)